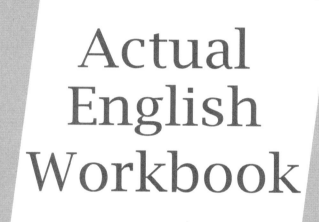

Actual English Workbook

Contents

1 Write three sentence about you and draw a picture of yourself.

"Hi. My name is Stacy. I live in Montreal. I'm Canadian."

_____

_____

_____

2 Write a list including your country and four other countries in alphabetical order.

_____

_____

_____

_____

ABCDEFGH
IJKLMNO
PQRSTU
VWXYZ

3 Complete the tables.

Singular	
I am	_I'm_
_____	You're
he is	_____
_____	she's
it is	_____

Plural	
_____	We're
you are	_____
	they're

4 Write sentences from the given information.

Sean / Irish / Limerick   Sean is Irish. He lives in Limerick.

Erica / American / New York   _____

Alan and Maggie / English / Manchester   _____

Craig / Australian / Canberra   _____

Todd and Gary / South African / Pretoria   _____

1 Solve the arithmetic problems. Write the answers in words.

two + five =   _seven_   eleven + two =   _____

ten × two =   _____   five × three =   _____

eighteen − nine = _____   twelve + eight =   _____

four × four =   _____   twenty − seven = _____

2 Look at the picture and write sentences about the people.

_____ _Daniel is 12._ _____   _____

3 Complete the statements with the correct form of the verb to be.

1 Complete the occupations puzzle.

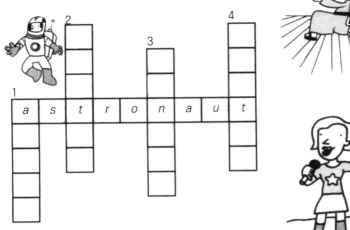

2 Complete the sentences with the correct form of the verb to be and a or an.

Ricky Martin *is a* singer. He _____ Puerto Rican.

Zinedine Zidane and Marcel Desailly _____ soccer players. They _____ French.

J. K. Rowling _____ writer. She _____ English.

Ben Affleck _____ actor. He _____ American.

I _____ student. I _____.

3 Match the pairs of numbers.

60	90		Thirteen	80
sixteen		nineteen	thirty	18
	30	sixty		19	ninety
16		eighteen	eighty	13

4 Read the dialog and complete the application form.

Librarian: What's your name?
Student: Jamie Hewitt.
Librarian: How old are you?
Student: I'm fourteen.
Librarian: What's your address?
Student: 236, Hillcrest Lane.
Librarian: And what's your telephone number?
Student: It's 281-4402.
Librarian: And your e-mail address?
Student: It's jamieh@santamonica.com

Willowdale Public Library
APPLICATION FORM

First name: _____
Last name: _____
Age: _____
Address: _____
Telephone: _____
E-mail: _____

1 Unscramble the names of the classroom objects and label the pictures.

kobo arctalluco urlre nep raseer lipnec speenharr botekoon

_____ _____ _____ _____

_____ _____ _____ _____

2 Complete the instructions with the correct verbs.

_____ down, please.

_____ your notebooks.

_____ the ruler, please.

_____ to the blackboard.

1 Read the information on the identification cards and complete the sentences.

Annual "Be a Good Student"
III *Conference*
Name:
Thomas Milne
Age:
14
Nationality:
South African

Annual "Be a Good Student"
III *Conference*
Name:
Mathilde Duchamps
Age:
13
Nationality:
French

Annual "Be a Good Student"
III *Conference*
Name:
Fernanda Ortiz
Age:
15
Nationality:
Colombian

Hi. My name's Thomas Milne.

I'm _____ years old.

I'm from _____.

Hi. _____.

I'm _____.

_____.

Hi. _____.

_____.

_____.

2 Write about a friend and draw his / her picture

_____
_____
_____
_____
_____

This is my friend.
Her name is Karla.
She is Venezuelan. She lives in
Caracas. She is 13
years old.

3 Underline the "odd one out" in each line.

actor	doctor	ruler	writer	basketball player
French	Ireland	Canadian	Mexican	Brazilian
he	I	live	they	we
door	four	seven	ten	twenty
eraser	notebook	calculator	pen	astronaut

4 Write your part of a conversation with Angela.

Angela: Hello. My name's Angela. What's your name?

You: _____

Angela: That's a nice name. How do you spell it?

You: _____

Angela: I'm fifteen. How old are you?

You: _____

Angela: I live in New York. Where do you live?

You: _____

Angela: What's your address?

You: _____

Angela: What's your telephone number?

You: _____

5 Complete the crossword puzzle.

Across

2. Hi. My _____ is Melissa.
4. Please _____ the door.
5. Fifty + ten = _____.
6. She's from Ireland. She's _____.
8. They are_____ Canada.
10. He is fifteen _____ old.
13. twelve, _____, fourteen fifteen, etc.
15. She lives in Houston. She's _____.
16. His name is Mark. _____ is my friend.

Down

1. Hi. I'm Dave. What's _____ name?
3. Carlos is from Mexico City. He's _____.
7. What's _____ last name?
10. Where do _____ live?
12. They are from Paris. They are _____.
14. This is a pencil and this is a _____.

9. Please _____ your books.
11. _____ down, class.
15. Tom Cruise is _____ actor.

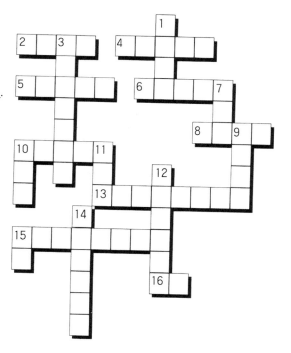

1 Complete the expressions with the correct word from the box.

brother   grandparents   parents   sister

She is my _____.

He is my _____.

We are his _____.

They are her _____.

2 Use the illustrations to complete the sentences below.

My aunt's children are my _____.

My father's parents are my _____.

My mother's brother is my _____.

My father's sister is my _____.

3 Look at the pictures and complete the questions and answers for your own family.

Do you have any sisters?   _____.

Do you _____ any brothers?   _____.

How many cousins _____ you have? _____.

4 Answer the questions with your information.

What's your name?   _____ name is _____.

What's your father's name?   _____ name is _____.

What's your teacher's name?   _____.

What's your best friend's name? _____.

1 Circle the correct word in parentheses in the following sentences.

Would you like one of (this / these) pieces of gum?

I am sending (that / those) card to my grandmother.

(That / This) red car on the other side of the parking lot belongs to my sister.

Have you seen (this / those) picture of my dad?

Whose umbrellas are (this / these)?

2 Change the following sentences as needed.

Singular	Singular
This is my brother.	_____
That is her cousin.	_____
_____	These are his sisters.
_____	These are our grandmothers.

3 Follow the lines to see who owns what. Then complete the questions and answers.

Whose _____ is it?
It's Grandpa's.

Whose glasses are _____?
They're _____.

Whose _____ is it?
_____ _____ Ben's.

Whose _____?
They're _____?

_____ CDs are _____?
They're _____?

1 Look at the different kinds of TV programs. Then complete the sentences with your information.

News

Talk Show

Sci-Fi Programs

Documentary

Sports

Cartoons

I like _____.

My mother hates _____.

(father / love) _____.

(sister / like) _____.

(grandmother / love) _____.

2 Read the paragraph and complete it with the words from the box.

don't like   sports   programs   comedies   rock   hates   likes   loves

My family fights every evening. We all like different TV _____. My mother _____ comedies, but my father _____ them. He wants to watch _____ programs. My brother _____ to watch _____ concerts, but I _____ music on TV. My mother always wins! And we all watch _____.

3 Look at the pictures and fill in the blanks.

_____ they like rock concerts?

Yes, _____.

_____ romantic movies?

Yes, _____.

_____ the children _____ horror movies?

No, _____.

1 Look at the pictures and answer the questions.

What does John like doing?

_____

What do the children like doing?

_____

What do they like doing?

_____

What does she like doing?

_____

2 Find five hobbies in the word chain.

fdwgfrgfishingñdodwalwcyclingqidemcaoijreadingerijgfdbpaintingasdfjhwatchingtvasdfgghjklper

3 Look at the pictures and complete the sentences. Use and, but, or or.

He likes fishing and listening to the radio.

She loves _____ she doesn't like _____ or _____.

You don't _____.

I don't _____.

We _____.

4 Answer the questions with your information.

Do you prefer reading the newspaper or a music magazine?   _____.

Does your mother prefer watching a movie or listening to music?   _____.

Does your father prefer watching sport or playing sport?   _____.

1 Complete the sentences with the correct word in parentheses.

Howmany brothers _____ you have? (does / do)

Ann _____ any cousins. (has / doesn't have)

They _____ two uncles. (have / has)

He _____ one sister and one brother. (have / has)

2 Circle the correct word in the following sentences.

You are the new student. What's his / her / your / name?

Is she in our class? What's his / her / our / name?

His / Her / Your / name is Tina. Her / She / You / is Steve's sister.

What are your parents' names? His / Her / Their / names are Pete and Martha.

3 Write your part of the conversation.

Hello, my name is Steve. What's your name?

_____

My parents' names are Shaun and Jessica. What are your parents' names?

_____

I have one sister. Her name is Tina. Do you have a sister?

_____

I don't have any brothers. And you?

_____

4 Write the names of classmates who fit in these situations.

_____ doesn't have any brothers.

_____ doesn't have any sisters.

_____ parents have three children.

_____ has two pets.

_____ father is a _____ .

5 Complete the questions about Bob's and Jackie's possessions. Write the answers.

Is that Jackie's skateboard?   No, it's Bobs.

_____?   _____.

_____?   _____.

_____?   _____.

_____?   _____.

6 Look at the pictures and write what the people like doing.

They like dancing.

_____   _____

_____   _____   _____

_____   _____   _____

7 Unscramble the sentences.

you / dance? / Do / to / like   _____

but / I do, / sister / my / doesn't.   _____

My / dancing / a lot. / likes / mother   _____

1— Look at the picture. Then read the sentences below and circle True or False.

There isn't a TV.	True	False
There is a computer on the bed.	True	False
The desk is under the window.	True	False
There are some books.	True	False
The bed is between the stereo and the door.	True	False
There aren't any CDs.	True	False
The closet is opposite the window.	True	False

2— Answer the questions in complete sentences.

Where is the cat? _____

Where are the CDs? _____

Where is the basketball? _____

Where is the lamp? _____

Where are the sports posters _____

Where is the stereo? _____

1 — Decode the names for parts of a house.

a = ✔ b = ✈ c = ❑ d = ❤ e = ☆ g = ■ h = ❝ i = ⇨ k = ❗ l = ★ m = Ⓒ n = ● o = ☞ r = ✖ t = ➤

✈ ✔ ➤ ❝ ✖ ☞ ☞ Ⓒ

_____

✈ ☆ ❤ ✖ ☞ ☞ Ⓒ

_____

❗ ⇨ ➤ ❑ ❝ ☆ ●

_____

■ ✔ ✖ ✔ ■ ☆

_____

❤ ⇨ ● ⇨ ● ■ ✖ ☞ ☞ Ⓒ

_____

2 — Complete questions and answers with is, isn't, are, or aren't.

Client: Is there a garage?

Realtor: Yes, there _____.

Client: Is there an elevator?

Realtor: No, there _____.

Client: How many bedrooms _____ there?

Realtor: There _____ two bedrooms.

Client: Is there any furniture in the dining room?

Realtor: Yes, there _____. There _____ a table.

Client: _____ there any chairs?

Realtor: No, there _____.

3 — Write three items in each list of household objects and furniture.

kitchen	living room	bathroom

1 Study the map and underline the false statements.

The library is between the hotel and the department store.

The bank is opposite the gas station.

The high school is on the corner of Mill Street and Wylie Street.

Mario's restaurant is on Central Boulevard next to the supermarket.

The parking lot is on the corner of Madison Street and Mill Street.

The hotel is next to Moore's department store.

2 Write sentences describing the location of these places.

The gas station

The police station

The supermarket

The hotel

3 Use the map to complete the dialog.

Visitor: Excuse me. Is there a bank near here?

Resident: Yes, there is. There's one on _____. It's opposite the

_____.

Visitor: Are there any _____ near here?

Resident: Well, there's one. It's on Madison Street, _____ the parking lot and the library.

Visitor: Is there an ice rink in this town?

Resident: Yes, there is. It's on the corner of _____ and _____.

Visitor: And where's the _____?

Resident: It's on Central Boulevard, next to the bank.

1 — Unscramble the requests. Be careful! There is <u>one</u> extra word.

I / your / please? / Could / my / borrow / ruler,

_____

please? / pen / you / help / me, / Could

_____

we / Could / wait / please? / use/ telephone, / the

_____

light / Could / turn / table / the / on, / please? / you

_____

your / you / please? / lend / Could / book, / me / write

_____

2 — Write the correct warning from the box under each picture.

> Be careful! It's unsteady.　　Watch out! The floor is wet.　　Don't touch it! It's hot.

_____　　_____　　_____

3 — Write an appropriate warning for each picture.

　_____　_____　

　_____　_____　

1 Read the description and draw the missing objects in each room.

In my house, there are two bedrooms. In my bedroom there is a bed, of course, and a closet. There are lots of books in a bookcase under the window. There is a table next to the bed. My computer is on the table. In my mom and dad's bedroom, there is a bed and two nightstands(one on each side). There is a large closet next to one nightstand. In the bathroom, there is a bathtub, a toilet, a shower, a wash basin, and a cupboard over the wash basin. In the living room there is a couch, two armchairs, a TV, and a lamp. In the dining room there's a table and four chairs. In the kitchen there is a refrigerator, cupboards, a stove, and a sink. There isn't a dishwasher. I'm the dishwasher!

2 Write sentences about what there is (or isn't) in your house or apartment.

In my bedroom there is _____

In the living room there is _____

In the kitchen _____

In the bathroom _____

3 Study the map and write the questions and answers.

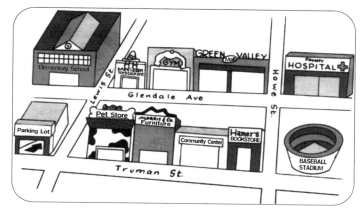

Q: Where's the pet store?

A: _____

Q: _____

A: It's on the corner of Glendale and Howe. It's opposite the shopping mall.

Q: Where's the gymnasium?

A: _____

Q: _____

A: It's on Glendale, between the pet store and the Community Center.

4 Number the parts of the dialog in the correct order.

_____ Thanks a lot.

_____ Where exactly?

___1___ Excuse me. Is there a bank near here?

_____ It's next to...er...Lacey's department store, opposite
the library.

_____ You're welcome.

_____ Yes, there is. There's one on Mayville Avenue.

5 Match the warnings with the correct pictures.

Careful! It's very spicy!   There's a spider in your soup!   Don't sit! The paint is wet!

1 Look at the refrigerator door and complete the questions and answers.

Are there any eggs? Yes, there are four.

_____ any butter? _____ .

_____ any ketchup? _____ .

_____ any milk? _____ .

_____ any bread? _____ .

2 Follow the example to complete the sentences.

What do you need to prepare popcorn at home?

I need a microwave oven.

What do you need to prepare a sandwich?

_____

What do you need to fix a glass of chocolate milk?

_____

What do you need to fix your cereal for breakfast?

_____

What do you need to make instant coffee?

_____

3 Rewrite the following sentences adding to where necessary.

Ice-cold lemonade

First, we need add sugar to the water. _____

Then you need add the lemon. _____

Use the large spoon stir. _____

Add some ice the mixture. _____

Now, it's ready serve. _____

1 Write questions for each picture. Then use the correct answer from the box.

There is a little   There is a lot   There are a lot   There are a few

How _____? _____.

How _____? _____.

How _____? _____.

How _____? _____.

Juice

2 Read the definitions and unscramble the words. Then write them in the correct column.

a) white liquid that babies love (kilm)

b) black drink that keeps you awake (fecfeo)

c) orange vegetable with a lot of vitamin A (rrctao)

d) popular Chinese food (crei)

e) vegetable that makes you cry (niono)

f) fruit that monkeys like (nabana)

Count nouns	Noncount nouns

3 Look at the pictures, read the sentences and circle True or False according to the situation.

How much ice cream is there?

There is a little.   True   False

How Much juice is there?

There is a little.   True   False

How many grapes are there?

There are a few.   True   False

How much cheese do we need for the pizza?

We need a lot.   True   False

1 Find four different stores in the wordsearch.

b	a	k	e	r	y	g	e	b	c	r
v	a	e	h	b	a	k	e	u	y	g
l	p	a	o	o	t	j	s	t	c	g
m	a	r	k	e	t	g	h	c	l	l
c	a	n	o	e	k	n	g	h	g	b
n	b	u	t	c	r	e	r	e	n	a
h	j	y	a	r	a	k	l	r	n	n
s	u	p	e	r	m	a	r	k	e	t

2 Match the columns.

_____Ingredients for a salad   A. apple

_____Beef from cattle   B. lettuce, tomatoes, carrots

_____A fruit that grows on trees.   C. potato

_____A vegetable that grows underground   D. steak

3 Complete the following dialogs in pairs.

A: Can I help you?
B: Yes, _____?
A: _____$ 1.50 a pound.
B: _____.

A: May I help you?
B: How _____?
A: _____.
B: _____.

A: _____ you?
B: _____ some avocados. How _____?
A: _____.
B: Please give me _____.

1 Look at the picture and complete the dialog.

Waiter: May I get you something to drink?
Boy:　　Yes, please.
Waiter: What would you like?
Boy:　　I want _____
Waiter: And you, Ma'am?
Mother: _____
　　　　(Waiter brings the drinks.)
Waiter: Are you ready to order?
Boy:　　Yes, I'd like _____
Waiter: And you?
Boy:　　_____
Waiter: Would you like dessert?
Mother: _____
Boy:　　_____
Waiter: Will that be all?
Mother: Yes, thank you.

2 In paris, discuss the foods and fill in the chart.

ice cream

bananas and apples

potato chips and dip

vegetable soup

boiled potato

water

soda

Healthy	Not Healthy

3 Match the questions and answers.

Would you like a glass of lemonade?　　　　Two.
Do you eat salad every day?　　　　　　　　8 glasses.
How much coffee do you drink?　　　　　　A little.
How many apples do you eat a day?　　　　Yes, I do.
How much water do you drink a day?　　　　Yes, please.

1 Look at the list and check (✔) the food that is on the table.

apples
hot dogs
salt
tomatoes
carrots
juice
lemons
bread

2 Find six hidden food items in the picture. Then write their names on the lines.

_____

_____

_____

_____

_____

_____

_____

3 Match each word with its correct measurement word.

butter	pound
juice	box
tomatoes	loaf
bread	stick
cereal	quart

4 Underline the correct words in the dialog.

Alice: Well, the party's almost over.

Tom: There (is / are) still (some / any) guests here and in the back yard.

Alice: (Are / Is) there (any / a few) soda left?

Tom: No, there (aren't / isn't) (any / some).

Alice: What else do we have? Tom: We have (a few / some) chocolate cake and (a little / a few) ice cream. How about potato chips?

Alice: No, we don't have (a few / any).

Tom: Let's call the store and order more soda and potato chips.

Alice: Good idea!

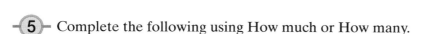

5 Complete the following using How much or How many.

_____ cups of coffee do you drink? A cup or two a day.

_____ is the coffee? It's 95 cents.

_____ sugar do you want in your coffee? Just a spoonful, please.

_____ cream would you like? No cream, thank you.

_____ pieces of toast? Three, please.

6 Look at the pictures and underline the correct answers.

How many CDs do they have for the party? They have (a few / a lot).

How (much / many) salad is there? There is (some / a few)

How (many / much) bread is there? There is (a little / a lot).

1 Complete the sentences with the correct events from the box.

shot put   javelin   400 meters   hurdles

He can jump the _____.

They can run the _____.

She can throw the _____.

He can throw the _____.

2 Study the table and write sentences about what people can and can't do.

	Jamie	Polly	Brad
do a cartwheel	✓	✓	x
climb a rope	x	x	✓
do a somersault	✓	✓	✓
do a handstand	x	x	x
do pushups	x	✓	✓

Jamie can _____

He can't _____

Polly can _____

She can't _____

Brad can _____

He can't _____

2 Write sentences about things that you can and can't do.

I can _____

I know how to _____

I'm good at _____

I can't _____

I don't know how to _____

I'm not very good at _____

1— Write the correct activity from the box under each picture.

ride a bicycle   play table tennis   skate   pitch a baseball   play golf

_____   _____   _____

_____   _____

2— Look at the pictures and answer the questions.

Can he skateboard?   Yes, he can.   Can he surf?

Can he dive?

Can they skate?

3— Look at the chart and complete each sentence with the correct verb.

Class 7B Sports Survey - Number of Students who can:										
swim	O	O	O	O	O	O	O	O	O	O
skateboard	O	O	O	O	O	O	O	O		
play tennis	O	O	O	O	O	O				
dive	O	O	O							
surf										

Most of the students in 7B can _____.   All of the students can _____.

Some of them can _____.   A few of them can _____.

None of them can _____.

1 Write A if the sentence is about ability or P if it is about possibility.

My sister can ride a bicycle.   A

You can run at the stadium.   _____

Look, there's a tennis court. We can play tennis.   _____

Can you do a handstand?   _____

I can swim but I can't dive.   _____

There are two diving boards. You can dive from 3 meters or from 5 meters.   _____

2 Use the table to write five sentences about sports activities and the places you can do them.

				play	tennis
	gymnasium	ice rink		skate	basketball
	running track	soccer field		swim	soccer
At the	swimming pool	baseball field	you can	lift	badminton
	diving pool	basketball court		dive	hockey
	tennis court	badminton court		run	weights
				work out	baseball

At the gymnasium you can lift weights.

_____

_____

_____

_____

3 Select three sports and write sentences about what you need to play each one.

To play hockey you need a stick, some skates, a
helmet, and special protective clothes.

_____

_____

_____

_____

_____

_____

1 Match the games with the objects.

chess

solitaire

backgammon

dominoes

checkers

2 Unscramble the questions and answers.

Q: play / do / chess? / What / need / to / you

_____

A: a / and / need / a set / of / You / chess pieces. / chessboard

_____

Q: people / many / play / do / How / you / to / bridge? / need

_____

A: play / people. / need / bridge / To / four / you

_____

Q: object / Monopoly? / is / of / What / the / game / the

_____

A: to / the most / is / object / money! / The / win

_____

3 Write about your favorite game. Use the notes to help you.

_____

_____

_____

_____

_____

_____

_____

My favorite game
• name of game?
• type of game? (word game, number game, etc)
• how many players?
• special equipment? (board, dice, pieces, etc.)

1 — Underline eight sports verbs in the racetrack.

START sjeotruridesjhekswimsjehksurfqowiujdiveshdjskatesjekfplaygjkorpethrowsjhegkjumpshjhekujf FINISH

2 — Use the verbs in Exercise 1 to write sentences about what you can and can't do.

I can skate.

_____

_____

_____

_____

3 — Complete the questions and answers.

Can he swim?

_____

No, she can't.

Can he surf?

_____

Yes, he can.

4 — Answer the questions about you and people that you know.

Can you dive?

Can you do a handstand?

Can your grandmother surf?   _____

Can your mother and father skate?   _____

Can your teacher swim?   _____

Can your best friend play tennis?   _____

Can your father ride a bicycle?   _____

5 Write to a friend about the sports you can play where you live.

_____

_____

_____

_____

_____

_____

You can swim at the swimming pool at the Sports Center. We can't skate because there isn't an ice rink...

6 Draw a line to match each object with the correct sport.

baseball

football

soccer

hockey

tennis

golf

7 Use the information in Exercise 6 to write sentences about what you need to play different sports.

To play golf you need _____

_____

_____

_____

_____

8 Underline the "odd one out" in each line.

play	jump	throw	javelin	pitch
ball	high jump	bat	racket	helmet
shot put	javelin	chess100	meters	discus
dice	court	rink	field	pool

1 Complete the clocks and the sentences below.

It's _eight thirty_ .   It's a quarter to six.   _____   It's ten after four.   _____

2 Look at the pictures and write sentences about Billy's routine.

He gets up at seven thirty.   _____   _____

_____   _____   _____

3 Complete the table with the correct verb forms.

I/ You / We / They	come	watch	go	study	have	work
He / She / It	comes					

4 Write about your daily routine.

I get up at _____

_____

_____

_____

_____

1 Complete the You column in the chart.

> always = +++++   usually = ++++   often = +++
> sometimes = ++   occasionally = +   never = —

	Beth	Steve	Beth	You
get up early	++++	+++++	+	
make breakfast for the family	+	+++	++	
go to school by bus	—	+++++	++++	
watch TV in the evenings	+++++	++	++++	
go to bed at ten o'clock	++	—	+++	

2 Now choose two people from the chart and write three sentences about their routines.

Beth often gets up early.

_____

_____

_____

_____

3 Complete each sentence with the correct form of the given verb.

My sister Cathy is so perfect! She always _gets up_ at six thirty. I always
_____ late.

She often _____ breakfast on Sundays. I never _____ breakfast.

I usually _____ my homework in the evening. She always _____ hers after
school.

She sometimes _____ TV for an hour or two. I often _____ TV all afternoon.

I sometimes _____ to bed at eleven thirty! She always _____ to bed early.

get up
make
do
watch
go

4 Complete each question with Do or Does. Then answer the questions.

_____ you get up early every day?   _____

_____ your dad wash the dishes?   _____

_____ your best friend go to the movies on weekends?   _____

_____ your mom and dad get up early?   _____

_____ you finish your homework every day?   _____

_____ your teacher sometimes come to class late?   _____

1 Complete the crossword with the days of the week.

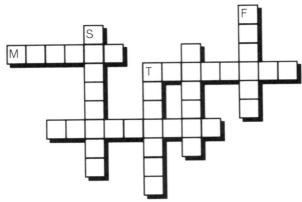

2 On the lines below write the days of the week in the correct order starting with Sunday.

_____

_____

3 Match the school subjects with the pictures.

1. Geography
2. Math
3. Physical Education
4. Art
5. History
6. Spanish

4 Write sentences about your class schedule.

English: _We have English on_ _____

Math: _____

Science: _____

_____ : _____

5 Complete the sentences about your favorite days of the week. Give reasons.

I like _____ because we have _____

I don't like _____

My favorite day of the week is _____

1 Unscramble the names of the months.

❑ B U R Y A R E F   *FEBRUARY*   ❑ B R E O C O T   _____

❑ A M Y   _____   ❑ L Y U J   _____

❑ M E R E D C E B   _____   ❑ M E E T B R E P S   _____

❑ N U E J   _____   ❑ L I P A R   _____

❑ C H A R M   _____   ❑ M E N B O V E R   _____

❑ U N Y J A R A   _____   ❑ U S U G T A   _____

2 Number the months above in the correct order.

3 Complete the sequences of numbers.

second	third	fourth	_____
tenth	eleventh	_____	thirteenth
sixteenth	seventeenth	eighteenth	_____
twenty-seventh	_____	twenty-ninth	_____

4 Look at the notes and complete the mini-dialogs about the celebrities' birthdays.

Q: When is Britney Spears' birthday?
A: It's on _____*December 2nd*_____.

Q: When is _____?
A: _____.

Q: _____?
A: _____.

Q: _____?
A: _____.

Q: _____?
A: _____.

Britney Spears
12/2/81

Ricky Martin
12/24/71

Drew Barrymore
2/22/75

Ben Affleck
8/15/72

Jennifer Lopez
7/24/70

5 Write complete sentences about the dates of four public holidays in your country.

_____

_____

_____

_____

_____

1 — Unscramble the sentences and complete the notes about Peter's daily routine.

at / ten / go / to / I / usually / o'clock. / bed

_____

to / twenty / I / eight. / at / past / school / go

_____

eight / breakfast / I / at / o'clock. / have

_____

I / seven / always / at / get / o'clock. / up

_____

lunch / have / at / one / I / school / o'clock. / at

_____

about / at / quarter / dressed / I / eight. / to / get

_____

My Day

get up - _____
get dressed - _____
have breakfast - _____
go to school - _____
have lunch - _____
go to bed - _____

2 — Complete the sentences about you, your family, and your friends.

After school, I usually   *go to my friend's house.*

My family often _____

I never _____

My friends sometimes _____

We occasionally _____

3 — Write appropriate questions using Do or Does.

Do you get up early?   Yes, I do. I always get up at six thirty.

_____   No, they don't. They go to school by bus.

_____   No, he doesn't. His mom usually makes breakfast.

_____   Yes, they always help around the house.

_____   No, she doesn't. She never does homework on Sundays.

4 — Answer the questions with short answers (Yes, I do. or No, I don't., etc.). Be honest!

Do you usually go to bed early?   _____

Do you always do your English homework?   _____

Do you make your won bed?   _____

Do you sometimes make breakfast for your family?   _____

Do you watch TV for more than two hours every day?   _____

5 Unscramble the words in the box and then write them in the correct categories.

phoggyrae	corboet	tesyadu	roshity
swayndeed	thenveesnet	inecsec	beetmerps
cednos	hegslin	thitwenet	nuadsy
najaury	dustraya	thinn	venromeb

School Subjects	Days	Months	Ordinal Numbers
Science	Sunday	January	twentieth

6 Complete the sentences.

Today is (month)_____, (day)_____, (year)_____.

My birthday is on _____.

Right now, it is (time) _____.

7 Look at the timetables and write the questions and answers.

When does Gary have Science?

On Tuesdays, Thursdays, and Fridays.

_____

_____

_____

_____

_____

_____

Science				
M	T	W	Th	F
	✔		✔	✔

Gary

Spanish				
M	T	W	Th	F
✔		✔		✔

Lisa and Joanne

History				
M	T	W	Th	F
✔		✔	✔	

Louise

Art				
M	T	W	Th	F
				✔

Stephen and Mark

1 Describe the weather in the following places.

the Rocky Mountains

London

Hawaii

Chicago

During the winter, it is very _____ in the Rocky Mountains.

In the spring, London is _____.

In the summer, Hawaii is _____.

During the fall, the weather in Chicago is very _____.

2 Look at the map and describe the weather conditions.

What is the weather like?

In England _____.

In France _____.

In Germany _____.

In Switzerland _____.

In Russia _____.

3 Complete the sentences about the weather.

Today the weather is _____.

Yesterday the weather was _____.

What kind of weather do you like (rainy, dry, cool, hot) ? Why ?

_____.

1 Look at the pictures and write what these famous people are doing.

_____   _____   _____

2 Complete the paragraph with the verbs needed.

It's a beautiful Sunday. There are lots of people in the park. Many children are

_____ and _____ _____. Some are _____.

A group of girl is _____ _____ and _____ _____.

An old couple is _____ _____ and one woman is _____ _____

a picture.

3 Complete the table.

Infinitive form	-ing form
eat	
swim	
dance	
cycle	
play	

1 Complete the conversation with the words from the box.

playing video games   eating   sleeping (2x)   doing   are   having   is

Mom：Sandy, this is Mom. Is everything okay?

Sandy：Um...Well, I'm _____ my homework.

Mom：Good, _____ Peter and Paul _____?

Sandy：No, they're _____.

Mom：What? It's definitely too late for that. And Alex?

Sandy：He _____ _____ his supper.

Mom：Eating? At this time?

Sandy：Well, he's not exactly _____.

Mom：I want to talk to your father.

Sandy：Well, he's _____.

Write a postcard to a friend using the ideas from the box.

London
rainy
not / have / fun.
walk a lot
visit / museums
not / go / parties
not / meet / new people

1 Solve the crossword puzzle.

2 Look at the picture and describe what the people are wearing.
Then write what they need to wear in those situations.

The boy is wearing _____.   She is wearing _____.
He needs to wear _____.   She _____.
_____.   _____.

They are wearing _____.
They _____.
_____.

3 Look at the pictures and write the correct sentence under each one.

> The hat is too big. The dress is too short. The T-shirt is too small. The tie is too long.

_____   _____   _____   _____

1 Use the following information to complete the paragraph.

2 Match the clothes with the weather conditions.

A   B

_____ cold and snowy

_____ hot and humid

C   D

_____ rainy and windy

_____ bright and sunny

3 – Complete the sentences using the correct form of the verb to be and the -ing form of the given verb.

We (have) *are having* fun.

My sister (meet) _____ all of her ex-classmates.

My dad (buy) _____ presents for everybody.

If (not rain) _____.

I (wear) _____ shorts and a T-shirt.

She (do) _____ homework in her bedroom.

They (not go) _____ to the movies.

4 – Describe what people are doing in the following pictures. Use the -ing form of the given verb.

_____ (sleep)   _____ (play)

_____ (ski)   _____ (swim)

5 – Underline the "odd one out" in each line.

hat	scarf	coat	boots	sandals	gloves
hot	rainy	cheap	cool	cold	cloudy
glasses	snow	clouds	rain	sunshine	wind
reading	fishing	swimming	working	water skiing	cycling
tie	suit	sunny	dress	shirt	skirt

1 Write the letter that matches the description.

Short _____
Large build _____
Black hair _____
Long hair _____
Thin _____
Short blond hair _____

2 Write three characteristics of each person.

_____   _____   _____

_____   _____   _____

_____   _____   _____

3 Look at the pictures, read the information and complete the descriptions.

Name: Julia Roberts
Nationality: American
Occupation: actress
Hair: brown
Eyes: brown

Name: Michael Owen
Nationality: English
Occupation: football player
Hair: blond
Eyes: green

Her name _____.

She is _____.

She _____ hair,

and _____.

She _____.

His name _____.

He's _____.

He _____ hair,

and _____.

He _____.

1 Look at the pictures and describe the people. Use the adjectives from the box.

attractive   honest   sociable   competitive   lazy   friendly   patient   hardworking   sociable

What is she like?

What is she like?

What are they like?

What is he like?

2 Find and circle five adjectives in the word chain.

fgtjlmnaggressivebgertsastrangeredgrvsfriendlygacrteenergeticiopytgenerous

3 Write the adjectives from Exercises 1 and 2 in the correct column.

Positive	Negative

1 Write the questions for the answers.

Jackie: I need some information about Ben for the yearbook. He's your brother, right?

Sarah: Yes, what do you need to know?

Jackie: _____?

Sarah: On August 17th.

Jackie: _____?

Sarah: Leo.

Jackie: _____?

Sarah: He's intelligent and hard-working.

Jackie: _____?

Sarah: He's sometimes lazy.

2 Find the information and complete the fact sheets.

Name:	Marion Jones
Nationality:	American
Occupation:	Athlete
Date of birth:	_____
Astrological sign:	_____
Sign characteristics:	_____

Name:	Hugh Grant
Nationality:	English
Occupation:	Actor
Date of birth:	_____
Astrological sign:	_____
Sign characteristics:	_____

Your own famous character

Name:	_____
Nationality:	_____
Occupation:	_____
Date of birth:	_____
Astrological sign:	_____
Sign characteristics:	_____

1 Give advice for each problem.

A: Are you okay?

B: No, I have a headache and a stomachache.

A: Take _____

and _____ .

A: What's up?

B: I think I have a cold and fever.

A: Take _____

and drink _____ .

A: What's wrong?

B: My skin hurts. It's red and I feel hot.

A: Put _____

on the red parts of your body.

2 Read the doctor's notes and help the nurse to write the report.

Carol - Headache - Aspirin / one at night.
Peter - Stomach - hot herb tea.
Paul - Flu - bed / lot of liquids.
Ed - cough - Stop smoking.
Betty - can't sleep - No coffee.

Name	Problem	Advice
Carol	She has a headache.	Take one aspirin at night.

1 Look at the picture and match the people with the description.

_____ has short blond hair

_____ is tall.

_____ has black hair.

_____ is short.

_____ has blond curly hair.

2 Look at the following pictures and match the people with the adjectives.

energetic and adventurous   (   )

nice and beautiful   (   )

sociable and friendly   (   )

aggressive and mean   (   )

3 Unscramble the names of the astrological signs. Match them with the symbol.

acircpron _____

pisorco _____

squaaurui _____

astruu _____

4 Match the adjective with their opposites.

_____ nervous
_____ interesting
_____ sociable
_____ hardworking
_____ dishonest

A. boring
B. lazy
C. trustworthy
D. calm
E. shy

5 Write a question for each answer.

_____?

Her name is Molly.?

_____?

She's intelligent and friendly.?

_____?

She was born on January 17th.?

_____?

She's an Aquarius.

6 Give advice for each situation.

I am bored.   I am hungry, but I have to work.   I have to go out.

_____ _____ _____

1 Read Matt's diary for last week and answer the questions.

Where was Matt on Monday morning?

_____

Where was Matt on Saturday evening?

_____

Where was the personal appearance on Thursday?

_____

Where was Matt's grandma's birthday party?

_____

Who was Matt with on Friday?

_____

What time was the appointment at Ace Studios?

_____

Where was Matt eleven o'clock on Tuesday morning?

_____

MAY

13 Monday
Meeting with Tony Mills
Continental Records - 10:00 a.m.

14 Tuesday
Dentist !! - 11 a.m.

15 Wednesday
Filming of new video
Ace Studios - 7:00 am.!!

16 Thursday
Personal appearance at
Mega Records - 4:00 p.m.

17 Friday
Lunch with Vicky

18 Saturday
Appearance on the Late Night Show

19 Sunday
Grandma's 75th birthday party.
Laurie's house

2 Complete the questions with was or were and then answer them.

Where _____ you yesterday at three o'clock?   _____

Where _____ your teacher an hour ago?   _____

Where _____ you exactly one week ago?   _____

Where _____ your mom last Saturday at four thirty? _____

Where _____ your parents at this time yesterday?   _____

3 Write the years in numbers and in words.

eighteen seventy-eight	_____	1999	_____
two thousand and one	_____	1776	_____
nineteen sixty-two	_____	1492	_____
nineteen forty	_____	1969	_____

1 — Complete the spaces in the dialog.

Kevin: What's that, Pete?

Pete: It's one of my dad's old records. He calls them LPs.

Kevin: Wow! Let me see. The Velvet Underground? Who or what _was_ that?

Pete: The Velvet Underground _____ a band in the late 1960s.

Kevin: _____ they American?

Pete: Yes, they _____. They _____ from New York, I think.

Kevin: _____ they like the Beatles and the Rolling Stone?

Pete: No, they _____. I think they _____ kind of weird, you know?

Kevin: So, who _____ in The Velvet Underground? Anybody famous?

Pete: Do you know Lou Reed?

Kevin: Yeah. Well, I know the name... I think.

Pete: Well, he _____ the singer and the guitarist with the band. And there _____ a woman in the bands as well.

Kevin: Really?

Pete: Yeah. She's called Maureen Tucker. She _____ the drummer.

Kevin: So, what _____ they like? I mean, what _____ their music like?

Pete: Well, let's listen to the record. Hey, Kevin, do you know how to operate these old record players?

2 — Use the notes to write a paragraph about John Lennon.

_____

_____

_____

_____

_____

_____

_____

_____

John Lennon

Full name: John Winston Lennon

Place of birth: Liverpool, England

Date of birth: October 9, 1940

Occupation: singer, guitarist, songwriter, political activist

1 Study the table and answer the questions with Yes, there were. or No, there weren't.

Were there any car seat belts in 1960?

_____

Were there barcodes on products in the 1960s?

_____

Were there any portable calculators before 1970?

_____

Were there any Post-it® note in the 1960s?

_____

Were there lava lamps before the 1970s?

_____

Tetrapak milk carton(1951)

car seat belt (1959)

lava lamp (1963)

portable calculator (1967)

2 Write three sentences about what there was and what there wasn't in the year 1970.

In 1970 there were _____

but there weren't any _____

_____

_____

_____

_____

_____

_____

floppy disk (1971)

Post-it® note (1973)

barcode(1973) disposable contact lenses(1987)

3 Write about what there was, and what there wasn't when your parents were still in school.

When my parents were in school, there weren't any _____

_____

_____

_____

_____

_____

_____

1 Complete the questions in the box with was or were.

Who _____ Matthew's Southern Comfort?

What _____ Haight-Ashbury?

Who _____ Jimi Hendrix?

Who _____ the flower children?

What _____ Woodstock?

2 Write the questions from Exercise 1 in the correct spaces.

So how much do you know about the 1960s?
Check out our "groovy" Q & A.

Q: _____

A: This district in San Francisco, California was the cultural center of the hippies in the 1960s.

Q: _____

A: These were young people, especially hippies. Typical attitudes were a rejection of conventional society and promotion of love, peace, and simple, idealistic values.

Q: _____

A: It was a rock music festival held in August, 1969 near Bethel, a village in the state of New York. The original site was near Woodstock, another town in New York.

Q: _____

A: They were a band. Their leader was an Englishman called Ian Matthews. Their big hit was a Joni Michell song called Woodstock. It was hit in England in September, 1970-a year after the Woodstock festival.

Q: _____

A: He was a famous American electric guitarist who revolutionized rock and roll music. He also performed at the Woodstock festival.

3 Write a series of history questions and answers about the present decade.
Use the ideas in the box and your own ideas.

_____   the Internet

_____   CD-ROMs

_____   George W. Bush

_____   movies on DVD

_____   Backstreet Boys

_____   chat rooms

_____

1 Underline the correct verbs in parentheses.

Professor: Yes! My time machine works! It works! So, tell me, where(was / <u>were</u>) you, Marty?

Marty: First, I (was / were) in a strange land. There (was / were) no people and there (was / were) no buildings. There (was / were) nothing but dust and...er...rocks. Behind me there (was / were) a strange spaceship...)

Professor: Of course! It (was / were) the year 1969 and you (was / were) on the moon!

Marty: Wow!

Professor: And then where (was / were) you?

Marty: Then, I (was / were) in an enormous crowd. There (was / were) strange people with long hair.And there (was / were) this...er...weird music. It (was /were) really loud...

Professor: Ah, yes. I know! It (was / were) the year 1969 again and you (was / were) at Woodstock!

Marty: I was? Hey, groovy! Er...I mean...Cool!

2 Read the text about Martin Luther King Jr. and complete the information in the biography File.

1960s Biography File: Martin Luther King Jr.

Date of birth: _____

Born in: _____

First son of: _____

Occupation: _____

Leading figure in: _____

MARTIN LUTHER KING JR.
Martin Luther King Jr. was a leader in the civil rights movement in the United States in the 1960s. He was born in Atlanta, Georgia in 1929. He was the first son of Martin Luther King Sr., who was a Baptist minister. Martin Luther King Jr. was a Baptist minister at the age of eighteen. From 1954 he was a minister in Montgomery, Alabama.

3 Now use the notes in this Biography File to write a paragraph about John F. Kennedy.

1960s Biography File: John F. Kennedy

Date of birth: 1917

Born in: Brookline, Massachusetts

Second son of: Joseph P. Kennedy

World War II service: Us Navy

US president: 1960-1963

JOHN F. KENNEDY

_____

_____

_____

4 Complete the sentences about you.

In the year 2000, I was _____ years old.

I was in _____ grade at school.

My teacher was _____.

My hobbies were _____.

My favorite singer / band was _____.

My favorite movie stars were _____.

5 Find nine music words in the wordsearch.

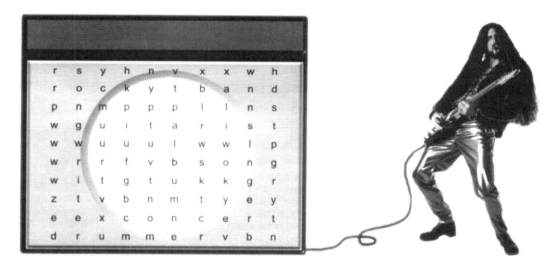

r	s	y	h	n	v	x	x	w	h
r	o	c	k	y	t	b	a	n	d
p	n	m	p	p	p	l	l	n	s
w	g	u	i	t	a	r	i	s	t
w	w	u	u	u	l	w	w	l	p
w	r	r	f	v	b	s	o	n	g
w	i	t	g	t	u	k	k	g	r
z	t	v	b	n	m	t	y	e	y
e	e	x	c	o	n	c	e	r	t
d	r	u	m	m	e	r	v	b	n

6 Unscramble the questions. Then answer them using complete sentences.

1960s? / games / there / the / any / Were / video / in

_____   _____

vinyl / Were / LP / there / the / in / 1970s? / records

_____   _____

there / the / e-mail / in / any / 1960s? / Was

_____   _____

telephones / there / Were / the / cellular / any / 1970s / in

_____   _____

Was / in / 1960s? / television / the / color / there

_____   _____

1 Unscramble the vacation-related words.

otru digeu _____   aspotprs _____   semumu _____

ssutmoc _____   tleoh _____   sterraanut _____

soirtut pma _____   hpipgnos _____

2 Now answer the questions using the words you unscrambled.

Where will you stay on your vacation?

_____

Where can you see art or historical destination?

_____

Who can show you around a tourist destination?

_____

What form of identification do you need to leave the country?

_____

What do you need to find places in the city?

_____

Where will you try the local cuisine?

_____

What could you do if you see some good deals in stores?

_____

3 Fill in the blanks with the past tense forms of the verbs from the box.

meet	go	invite	say	take	be
ride	eat	drink	want	sleep	drive

Christine and Harry _____ to Colombia last summer to visit their aunt.

On the first day of their vacation, they _____ motorbikes.

They _____ all over the city until they got hungry.

Then they _____ in a small restaurant. The food _____ great!

Later in the week their aunt _____ them to a small town in the countryside.

They _____ their aunt's friends and _____ delicious Colombian coffee.

Then they all _____ in hammocks.

Christine and Harry _____ sad when they had to leave.

They _____ to stay, but they had to go back to school.

Their aunt _____ them to come back next summer. They _____ , "Great idea!"

1 Find seven famous cities in Europe.

y	n	d	f	g	y	r	w	r	t
t	y	l	o	n	d	o	n	p	u
p	w	r	y	y	b	m	d	v	x
a	t	h	e	n	s	e	p	e	m
r	g	p	r	f	f	f	n	m	m
i	x	x	z	m	a	d	r	i	d
s	x	h	h	f	g	j	j	c	l
x	x	w	q	y	y	p	l	e	z
n	b	a	r	c	e	l	o	n	a

2 Match each picture with a sentence.

_____ First our plane arrived at the airport.

_____ Then we went to the hotel to check in.

_____ Later that day we explored the city.

_____ Finally we came back to the hotel and relaxed by the pool.

A

B

C

D

1 Read the questions and number the answers in the correct order.

A: Did you go on vacation this year? _____ B: Yes, he came to see me at the hotel.

A: Did Peter go with you? _____ B: Yes, I went to Cancun.

A: Did you have a nice time? _____ B: Yes, he gave me a shot.

A: Did you see a doctor? _____ B: No, we didn't go together.

A: Did he give you the right medicine? _____ B: No, I only saw the ocean from the hotel room!

A: Did you swim at all _____ B: No, I got sick on the first day.

2 Complete the letter using the correct past-tense forms of the given verbs.

Dear Laura,

My trip _____ not very good. We _____ some bad luck.
(be)   (have)

The airport _____ our luggage.
(lose)

My friend _____ to reserve a room at the hotel.
(forget)

The bank _____ sclosed for a holiday.
(be)

And a dog _____ me at the beach!
(bite)

Hopefully my next trip will be more fun and you'll come with me!

Love,
Peter

3 Reread the letter and number the pictures in order.

Actual English Workbook

1 — Use the illustrations to describe the vacation using the past tense.

Vacation in Paris

First _____

_____.

Then _____

_____.

That afternoon _____

_____.

Later _____

_____.

That evening _____

_____.

Finally _____

_____.

2 — Write the simple past-tense forms of the following verbs.

1. ski _____*skied*_____
2. swim _____
3. walk _____
4. buy _____

5. snorkel _____
6. dive _____
7. fly _____
8. see _____

3 — Now match the verbs with the illustrations.

_____   _____   _____   _____

_____   _____   _____   _____

1 Rewrite the sentences in the past tense.

Henry arrives at the airport.

Henry arrived at the airport

His flight is delayed.

_____

Because of the delay, Henry misses his connecting flight.

_____

He calls his family to tell them about the delay.

_____

His family leaves for the airport before Henry calls them.

_____

His family waits for him for several hours before his plane finally lands.

_____

2 Write a paragraph describing the game using first, then, and later.

Daniel went to a soccer game in Argentina.

_____
_____
_____
_____
_____
_____
_____
_____

3 Underline the "odd one out" in each line.

airplane	passport	bus	train	car
museums	shops	monuments	restaurants	reservation
water skiing	luggage	scuba diving	swimming	snorkeling
tour guide	flight attendant	delayed	hotel receptionist	travel agent
Riviera Hotel	France	Spain	Mexico	Italy

4 Write a question for each answer.

_____? We saw beautiful landscapes.

_____? We visited Chile and Brazil.

_____? We swam in the ocean and rivers.

_____? We ate fish and shrimp.

5 Write the simple past-tense forms of the verbs.

eat _____

go _____

swim _____

see _____

have _____

do _____

부록

1. Spoken American English(1)

Tape # 1

1. **Relaxation**(긴장풀기)

    1) **Breathing**   2) **Yawning**   3) **Stretching**   4) **Shaking**   5) **Swallowing**

2. **Tonal Action**(조성운동)

    1) eee[i;]   2) aaa[ei]   3) yyy[j]

    ex) : eee-yes   eee-you   eee-yesterday   eee-year

3. **Y-Buzz Siren**(Y 울림소리)

    1) **Y-initial position**(Y로 시작하는 단어) :

    Yellow   You   Yard   Yell   Yield   Yes   Use

    2) **Y-final position**(Y로 끝나는 단어) :

    Happy   Angry   Hungry   Thirsty   City   Ready

    3) **The Y sentences**(Y 문장연습) :

    a. I'm hungry and thirsty, and I'm not happy.

    b. I'm ready to yield to this city.

    c. Yes, I yelled across the yard.

    d. I'm angry that you used my yellow car.

    4) **E-word list**(E 단어연습) :

    He   She   We   Sweethearts   T-shirt

    Sleeves   Jeans   Reading   Argentina

    Trees   Green   Feet   Sleep   Meat   Cheese

    The E sentences(E 문장연습) :

    a. We sweethearts are reading about Argentina.

    b. He wore jeans and a t-shirt with short sleeves.

    c. Lying under a green tree, eating meat and cheese, his feet fell asleep.

    5) **+Y-buzz**(+Y울림소리) : E[e] plus EEE[i] = A

    a. yee-yee-yee-yee, now yee-yey-yee-yey...

    b. yee-yey-yee-yey, yey-yey-yey-yey-yey-yey.

    6) **A word list**(A 단어연습) :

    They   Name   David   Bathing suit   Cake

    Baby   Plate   Grapes   Table   Grey

    A sentences(A 문장연습) :

a. The baby in the grey bathing suit is named David.

b. They laid the table with plates of cake and grapes.

Tape # 2

1. Structural Action(구조 운동) : #1, #2, #3, #4, #5, #6

#1–OH[u;], #21–OH[ou], #3–O[ɔ], #4–AW[ɔ;], #5–AH[ɑ;], #6–A[æ]

2. Phonetic Alphabet(음성기호)

1) **Vowels**(모음)

[Y=i;]	see, beat, seat
[+Y=ei]	bay, aim, name
[AH=ɑ;]	calm, father, farm
[OO=u;]	boot, food, too
[O=ɔ]	long, dog, orange
[AW=ɔ:]	all, caught, saw
[OH=ou]	show, low, no
[OW=au]	cow, out, bound
[A=ɔ]	bat, hat, attic
[OY=ɔi]	boy, toy, coin
[I=ai]	time, sky, buy
[UR=ə;r]	bird, earn, burn
[oo=u]	good, put, full
[ih=i]	live, bit, ink
[eh=e]	bell, bet, end
[uh=ʌ]	love, up, just
[oor=uər]	poor, tour, moor
[eer=iər]	beer, ear, hear
[ear=eər]	bear, care, there
[our=ɔər]	bore, chore, more

2) **Consonants**(자음)

[N=n]	note, dinner, moon
[M=m]	man, summer, aim
[V=v]	vine, cover, love
[F=f]	fox, offer, if
[Z=z]	zoo, busy, lose
[S=s]	cent, fussy, kiss
[B=b]	bed, rubber, baby
[P=p]	pay, upper, cup
[D=d]	desk, rudder, good
[T=t]	top, better, tent
[G=g]	gum, beggar, big
[K=k]	call, lucky, desk
[TH=ð]	this, other, bathe
[TH=θ]	think, pithy, both
[ZH=ʒ]	casual, vision, rouge
[SH=ʃ]	ship, station, fish
[NG=ŋ]	ink, sing, king
[L=l]	leg, melon, call
[W=w]	way, wagon, wave
[Y=j]	yes, year, yell
[R=r]	rain, sorry, red
[H=h]	house, hand, behind
[DG=dʒ]	gem, judge, ridge
[CH=tʃ]	chair, pitcher, match
[DZ=dz]	ads, sounds, ends
[TS=ts]	hats, seats, minutes

3. **#5-AH[ɑ;]** as in father, calm

   1) **The #5 Word List**(#5 단어연습)

   Father, arm, car, bar, barn

   Calm, palm, star, yard, sweetheart

4. **#1-OO[u;]** as in you, blue

   1) **The #1 Word List**(#1 단어연습)

   You, blue, two, new, to

   Noon, excuse, shoe, spoon, moon

5. **#4-O[ɔ]** as in long, blonde

   1) **The #4 Word List**(#4 단어연습)

   Long, blonde, not, dollar, body

   Clock, block, sock, rock, box

6. **#3-AW[ɔ;]** as in ball, short

   1) **The #3 Word List**(#3 단어연습)

   Ball, short, four, forty, morning

   Forehead, laundromat, horse, saw, law

7. **#21-OH[ou]** as in no, don't

   1) **The #21 Word List**(#21 단어연습)

   Know, don't, go, shoulder, toe

   Nose, those, grow, phone, comb

8. **#51-OW[au]** as in now, brown

   1) **The #51 Word List**(#51 단어연습)

   Now, brown, how, eyebrow, thousand

   Hours, house, towel, flower, clown

9. **#6-A[æ]** as in black, eyelashes

   1) The #6 Word List(#6 단어연습)

   Hand, back, eyelashes, moustache, black

   Has, afternoon, half past, at, address

10. **#3Y-OY[ɔi]** as in boy, toy

   1) **The #3Y Word List**(#3Y 단어연습)

   Boy, toy, joy, soil, foil

   Oil, boil, coil, loin, annoy

11. #6Y-I[ai]   as in time

　1) The #6Y Word List(#6Y 단어연습)

　　I, time, my, white, eye, five, nine, dime, light, type

12. R-Vowel UR[ɔ;r]   as in shirt, work

　1) The R-Vowel Word List(R-Vowel 단어연습)

　　Work, shirt, her, thirty, thirteen

　　Curly, gird, earth, girl, skirt

13. Sentences for Structural Perception(구조개념 문장연습)

　1) Those five dollar blue jeans don't go at all badly with the flowered shirt you found at the laundromat.

　2) At exactly half past noon I used my hand to curl back my black moustache.

　3) Father calmly drove the brown car back from the barn down the palm-lined boulevard.

　4) The joyful boy was soiled with oil from coiling up with the annoying toy.

　5) The bird ate thirty earthworms.

　6) Her girlish skirt made the long blonde-haired thirteen-year-old every boys type.

　7) Excuse me, do you know the new address on this block for those shoulder-to-toe yard boxes saw advertised on TV?

Tape #4

　－Consonant Action(자음운동)

1. N(유성 치경 비음)

　a. Rain, on, fender, turn, between

　b. Department, one, phone, emergency, station

　c. There was rain on the fender.

　d. There was one telephone at the emergency station.

　e. Turn between the van and the fire department.

2. M(유성 양순 비음)

　a. Swim, team, from, welcome, ice cream

　b. Ambulance, number, come, arm, comb

　c. The swim team from Rome was welcomed.

　d. The ambulance number will come to mind.

　e. I got ice cream on my arm when I went for my comb.

3. **V**(유성 순치 마찰음)

　　a. Five, of, seven, sleeve, very

　　b. Leave, river, drive, move, stove

　　c. Five of seven sleeves are very long.

　　d. Did they leave the river for a drive?

　　e. Let's move the stove last.

4. **F**(무성 순치 마찰음)

　　a. Knife, leaf, half, finger, elephant

　　b. Laugh, off, telephone, fire, roof

　　c. I used a knife to cut the leaf in half.

　　d. When she touched her finger to the elephant I had to laugh.

　　e. I got off the telephone fast, when I saw the fire on the roof.

5. **Z**(유성 치경 마찰음)

　　a. These, moves, dials, those, gears

　　b. Wipers, rains, excuse, is, nose

　　c. These moves turn the dials.

　　d. Those gears run the wipers when it rains.

　　e. Excuse me, is my nose bleeding?

6. **S**(무성 치경 마찰음)

　　a. It's, face, this, office, close

　　b. Police, bus, stops, across, gas

　　c. It's a nice face.

　　d. This office is close to the police station.

　　e. The bus stops across from the gas station.

7. **B**(유성 양순 비음)

　　a. Baby, table, bib, boy, boat

　　b. Tub, bed, ribbon, hubcap, bird

　　c. The baby at the table has a bib.

　　d. The boy played with a boat in the tub.

　　e. Under the bed was a ribbon, a hubcap, and a live bird.

8. **Comparison the V with the B**(V와 B의 비교)

　　a. Vat-bat, veil-bail, vest-best, very-berry, vend-bend

　　b. Curves-curbs, marvel-marble, calve-cab, rove-robe, dove-dub

9. D(유성 치경 파열음)

   a. Stand, wood, bed, red, head

   b. Inside, windshield, bird, hand, outside

   c. Stand by the wood bed.

   d. She put her red head inside the windshield.

   e. A bird in hand is worth two outside.

10. T(무성 치경 파열음)

   a. Wait, start, front, that, post

   b. left, it, right, exhaust, at

   c. Wait-start in front.

   d. Take tat post to the left.

   e. It was right to exhaust many at once.

11. ED Endings(과거형 접미사 ED)

   a. Unvoiced : Ripped, tapped, kissed, missed, fished, cashed

   b. Voiced : handed, started

12. G(유성 연구개 파열음)

   a. Dog, pig. digging, burglary, egg

   b. Rug, ignition, green, wagon, flag

   c. The dog and the pig were digging.

   d. After the burglary I found an egg on the rug.

   e. The ignition was caused by the green wagon with the flag.

13. K(무성 연구개 파열음)

   a. Walk, block, back, park, thank

   b. Bank, sick, excuse, brake, trunk

   c. Walk one block back to the park.

   d. I can thank the bank for making me sick.

   e. Excuse me, but the brake shoe is not in the trunk.

14. PT Word List & Sentences(PT 단어연습 및 문장연습)

   a. Stopped, slept, roped, slipped, wiped

   b. We stopped and slept for a while.

   c. I roped off the area where she slipped, and wiped up.

15. KT Word List & Sentences(KT 단어연습 및 문장연습)

   a. Talked, act, backed, tucked, looked

b. We talked before the act that he backed.

c. I tucked mine away and locked up.

16. GD Word List & Sentences(GD 단어연습 및 문장연습)

a. Tugged, rigged, hugged, begged, bagged

b. I tugged the rope and rigged the mast.

c. She hugged me and begged for what I had bagged.

17. BD Word List & Sentences(BD 단어연습 및 문장연습)

a. Jabbed, ribbed, robed, grabbed, stabbed

b. We jabbed and ribbed him.

c. The robed man was grabbed from behind and stabbed.

Tape #5
–More Consonant Action(자음운동 2)

1. TH[ð](유성 치간 마찰음)

a. Father, with, those, there, this

b. Brother, these, clothes, that, the

c. Father is with those others in there.

d. This brother and these clothes go together.

e. That is the best.

2. TH[θ](무성 치간 마찰음)

a. Nothing, healthy, bath, three, things

b. Birthday, mouth, something, tooth, throat

c. There is nothing healthy about a cold bath.

d. He got three things for his birthday.

e. In my mouth, something from my tooth went down my throat.

3. SH[ʃ](무성 치경구개 마찰음)

a. Shirt, wash, fresh, fish, brush

b. Shoe, fashion, receptionist, push, shoulder

c. I took off my shirt to wash the fresh fish.

d. I brush my shoes and stay in fashion.

e. The receptionist pushed my shoulder.

4. ZH[ʒ](유성 치경구개 마찰음)

a. Measure, garage, usual, leisure, massage

b. Pleasure, casual, vision, rouge, treasure

c. Measure the garage the usual way.

d. For leisure I find massage a pleasure.

e. I had a casual vision: I saw a rouge treasure chest.

5. **NG [ŋ]** (유성 연구개 비음)

a. King, ring, tongue, swing, staying

b. Sing, nothing, wrong, swimming, string

c. The king had a ring through this tongue.

d. After the swing dance, she's staying to sing.

e. There's nothing wrong with swimming in a string bikini.

6. **NK : K Drumbeat**(K 두드림 소리)

a. Ink, honk, drunk

b. If I honk at the drunk he'll spill the ink.

7. **Medial NG : No G Drumbeat**(G 두드림 소리를 내지 않음)

a. Swinging, singer, hanged

b. The swinging singer was hanged.

8. **NG+Comparative/Superlative**: Play the G Drumbeat
   (NG+비교급/최상급 : G 두드림 소리를 냄)

a. Younger, stronger, longer

b. The younger woman was stronger and lasted longer.

c. Youngest, strongest, longest

d. The youngest man was strongest and lasted longest.

9. **Medial NG** : G/K Drumbeat(G/K 두드림 소리를 냄)

a. Anger, ankle, tangle

b. I felt anger when my ankle got tangled in the line.

c. 예외: 고유명사의 경우(Washington, Birmingham, Bingham)

10. **L**(유성 치경 설측음)

a. School, ball, hospital, file, list

b. Illness, cold, milk, ailment, feel

c. After school they played ball.

d. The hospital files list all my illnesses.

e. Drink cold milk for your ailment, and you'll feel better.

11. W(연구개 과도음)

a. Swimming, once, twice, waves

b. Sandwich, wagon, water, washing

c. I went swimming once or twice in the waves.

d. The sandwich wagon needs water for washing.

12. Linking W(연결음 W)

a.	1	y<u>ou</u>	<u>w</u>	are	[ju; <u>w</u> a;r]
b.	21	go	<u>w</u>	inside	[gou <u>w</u> insaid]
c.	51	now	<u>w</u>	enter	[nau <u>w</u> entər]

13. Y(치경구개 과도음)

a. Yellow, onions, yard

b. Yesterday, you, lawyer

c. I found yellow onions in the yard.

d. Yesterday you spoke to the lawyer.

14. The Y Link(연결음 Y)

a.	Y	he	y	insists	[hi y insists]
b.	+Y	today	y	is	[tudei y iz]
c.	3Y	employ	y	everyone	[evri y wən]
d.	6Y	lie	y	on it	[lai y nit]

15. R(치경 과도음)

a. Reporter, running, radio, waitress, photographer

b. Regular, carrying, red, refrigerator, raining

c. The reporter was running around the radio station.

d. The waitress brought the photographer his regular order.

e. I'm not carrying that red refrigerator while it's raining.

16. H(무성 성문 마찰음)

a. Hat, head, house, hair, hand

b. When, what, whistle, whisper, which[wh hw]

c. You need a hat on your head when you leave the house.

d. What boy whistled at her hair?

e. Whisper behind your hand which one.

17. DG[dʒ] (유성 치경구개 파찰음)

a. Job, orange, juice, cabbage, refrigerator

b. Garbage, engineer, badge, jumping, bridge

c. You did a good job squeezing the orange juice.

d. I took the cabbage from the refrigerator and threw it in the garbage.

e. The engineer wearing the badge saw someone jumping from the bridge.

18. CH [tʃ] (무성 치경구개 파찰음)

a. Check-up, chicken, kitchen, watch, teach

b. Church, cheese, lunch, match, chair

c. Check-up on the chicken while you're in the kitchen.

d. Watch others teach at the church.

e. The color of our cheese lunch matched the chair.

19. SH [ʃ] (무성 치경구개 마찰음)

a. Shop-chop, sheep-cheap, shoes-choose

b. Shopper-chopper, shared-chaired, cashes-catches

c. Mash-match, dish-ditch, wish-witch, crush-crutch

20. DZ (TS와 조음위치와 조음방법이 같은 동질음)

a. Husbands, hands, foods, sounds, roads

b. Ads, tends, finds, holds, ends

c. Her husband's hands mixed the foods.

d. The sounds on these roads have been used in many ads.

e. The gardener tends plants and finds a basket that holds ends.

21. TS (DZ와 조음위치와 조음방법이 같은 동질음)

a. Sports, hurts, parents, that's, carrots

b. Lights, paints, parts, what's, minutes

c. His dislike of sports hurts his parents.

d. That's where the carrots grow under lights.

e. The machine paints parts in what's minutes saved per part.

22. DL / TL

a. Needle, middle, puddle, cradle, medal

b. Little, bottle, rattle, dental, cattle

c. The little bottle caused a rattle.

d. There was a needle in the middle of the puddle under the cradle.

e. His dental work on cattle won him a medal.

23. The Medial DL / TL

a. Wildly, idling, boldly, worldly, endless

b. Restless, lately, correctly, exactly, perfectly

c. I've been wildly restless lately.

d. The engine is correctly idling at exactly the right speed.

e. He acted boldly and perfectly worldly, but I thought it was endless.

2. Hunting for English(2)

Video 1-1

Harrison : Hello?

Maeng : Who's calling(=speaking), please? (=To whom am I speaking?)
(=Who is this, please?)

Harrison : This is Harrison. Can I(=I want to, or I'd like to) speak to Mr. Lee?
(=Would you mind calling Mr. Lee to the phone?)

Maeng : Hold on a second.

Mr. Lee! There's a phone call for you.(=You are wanted on the phone)

cf. Mr. Kim wants you on the phone.

Are you here? I'm not here.

- Who's calling, please?= To whom am I speaking? - 누구시죠?
- Are you here? - 계시다고 할까요?
- I'm not here. - 없다고 하세요.
- Can I speak to Mr. Lee? - 미스타 리 좀 바꿔주겠어요?
- There's a phone call for you.= You are wanted on the telephone.
  – 전화 왔어요.

Video 1-2

Harrison : Hello?

Maeng : Who's calling, please?

Harrison : This is Mr. Harrison. Can I speak to Mr. Park?

Maeng : I'm sorry, he's not in(=here) now.

- He's out on business. - 그는 출장중 입니다.
- He's in conference now. - 그는 회의중 입니다.
- He's just stepped out.(=You've just missed him.) - 그는 방금 나갔습니다.
- He's gone(=left) for the day. - 그는 퇴근했습니다.

May I take a(=your) message?(=Will you leave a(=your) message?)

cf. Can you take a(=my) message?(=Can I leave a(=my) message?)

Video 1-3

Foreigner : Hello?

Maeng : Hello?

Foreigner : Can I speak to Mr. Wang?

Maeng : What number did you dial?(=What number are you calling?)

Foreigner : 457-7835

Maeng : The number is right. But there's nobody by that name.

- You got(=have) the wrong number. - 전화 잘못 걸었습니다.
- You are a wrong number.
- There's nobody by that name. - 그런 이름을 가진 분은 안 계십니다.

Video 1-4

Maeng : Hello?

Foreigner : Hello? Can I ask you where my budget forecasts are for the Mandarm files?

Maeng : Well, for that information, let me put you through to(with) Line 2.

(Let me put you through to Mr. Lee who is in charge.)

cf. Let me contact you with Line 2.

Foreigner : Wait a minute, please. I'm sorry, but the person in charge is not in now.

- Let me put you through to Mr. Lee who is in charge.
  - 담당자 미스타 리를 바꿔 드리겠습니다.
- Let me contact you with Line 2. - 2번을 연결해 드리겠습니다.

Video 1-5

Maeng : Hello? This is Mr. Maeng of Mirae Trading Company.

Can I speak to Mr. Kim?(I'd like to speak to Mr. Kim. / Is Mr. Kim there?)

Foreigner : I'm sorry, he's not in(=here) now.

Maeng : Is that right? Well, can you take my message for him?

- When will he be back? / When do you expect him back?
  - 그 사람이 언제 돌아올까요?
- May I speak to ~? = I'd like to talk to ~ = I want to speak to ~
  - 누구 누구 좀 바꿔 주겠습니까?
- May I take a(=your) message? =Will you leave a(=your) message?
  - 제가 메시지를 받아 드릴까요? = 메시지를 남기시겠어요?
- Can you take a(=my) message? =Can I leave a(=my) message?
  - 메시지 좀 받아주시겠어요? = 메시지를 남겨도 될까요?

Video 1-6

Maeng : Yes! Hello? Can I speak to Mr. Kim?

Foreigner : He's not in now. Can I take a message?

Maeng : Please tell him (that) I'll call back at about 12.

- Please tell him to call me at home/at office/at 555-5555.
  - 그 사람한테 집으로/사무실로/ 몇 번으로 전화하라고 전해주세요.
- Please tell him that I called to see If he could attend the meeting to night.
  - 그가 오늘밤 모임에 참석할 수 있는지 알아보려고 제가 전화했었다고 그에게 전해주세요.

Video 1-7

Maeng : Can I sit here?(Is someone sitting here? / Mind if I sit here?)

Foreigner : Sure.

Maeng : Thank you. The weather is nice, isn' t it?(How is the weather today?
What do you think about the soccer game?) Do you like the weather?

Foreigner : Yes. I really like it.

Maeng : Is this your first time to visit this place?

Foreigner : Yes. Can I talk to you for a minute?

- Can you give me a minute? - 잠시 시간 좀 내 주시겠어요?

Video 1-8

Maeng : Can(May) I sit here?(Is someone sitting here?/ Mind if I sit here?)

Foreigner : Sure!

Maeng : Are you here in Korea for business or pleasure?

Foreigner : For business.

Maeng : Can I ask you what kind of business?

Foreigner : It' s trading business between Korea and America.

Maeng : I see. Then you must come to Korea very often.

Foreigner : At least, once in a month.

- What' s your impression on Korea? - 한국에 대한 인상이 어때요?

Video 1-9

Maeng : How long have you stayed in Korea?

Foreigner : About 2 weeks.

Maeng : is that right?

Foreigner : Yes. I really like it.

Maeng : Good to hear that.
You have no problem getting around bay yourself?

Foreigner : No, I haven' t. But thank you for asking.

Maeng : My pleasure.

- Is that right? - 그렇습니까? / 그러세요?

Video 1-10

Maeng   : You are a student, I presume.

Foreigner : Yes.

Maeng   : What do you study in college?

foreigner : Business management.

Maeng   : Oh, I studied business management, too.

Are you visiting Korea during your vacation?

Foreigner : Yes.

Maeng   : I think it was a good choice.

Video 2-1

Maeng   : I started working for a trading company right out of(after) college.

I like my job. Are you satisfied with your major?

(Do you like your major?)

Foreigner : I like it. Business management is very fantastic.

Maeng   : Yes, it was. What are you planning to do after graduating? (What are your plans after graduation?) Do you want to get a job?

Foreigner : Yes.

Video 2-2

Maeng   : Oh, my God, it's about time. I've got to get back to my office.

Foreigner : Oh, I see.

Maeng   : Nice talking to you. I want to keep(get) in touch with you.

((It's been) nice meeting you.)

Can I have your phone number or address if you don't mind?(If it's O.K.?)

Foreigner : Sure. Here you are. This is my phone number.

Maeng   : Thank you. Have a good(nice) stay in Korea. Bye!

Video 2-3

Buyer   : Excuse me.

Maeng   : May I help you?(=What can I do for you?/So, you are Mr. Brown?)

Buyer   : I'm James Brown. I'm looking for ABC Trading Company.

Maeng   : Welcome. Nice to meet you. I'm Maeng.

Buyer   : Nice to meet you.

Maeng   : here's my card.

Buyer	: Thank you. Here's mine.
Maeng	: Oh, thank you. Have a seat, please.(=Please be seated.)
Buyer	: Yes.

Video 2-4

Maeng	: Would you care for(like) something to drink?
Buyer	: Coffee, please.
Maeng	: Oh, coffee. Did you come from the airport?
Buyer	: No. I came from my hotel.
Maeng	: How did you get(come) here?
Buyer	: By taxi.(On foot, By air, By subway, By ship, By train)
Maeng	: Oh, by taxi. how was the traffic? It was horrible, wasn't it?
Buyer	: Oh, yes. It was terrible. I'm so tired.
Maeng	: I understand. I don't blame you. You must have jet lag. Do you feel all right?
Buyer	: Yes, I'll be all right.

Video 2-5

Maeng	: O.K. Then let's get down to business(studying, talking). I'm ready if(whenever) you are. (Let's get start it on our business.)
Buyer	: I'm ready, too.
Maeng	: I think today's(our) discussion will go all right(smoothly).
Buyer	: Sure, it will.(I think so, too.)

Video 2-6

Maeng	: I think we are finished. Okay, it's a deal. I'm happy about the results.(Are you satisfied with our(the) result?)
Buyer	: So am I.
Maeng	: Let's drink to that tonight(Let's go out for a drink tonight), if you don't mind.
Buyer	: Great idea!
Maeng	: Let's get going.

Video 2-7

Maeng	: Well, our discussion was very productive.(We had a very productive discussion.) Let's talk about it tomorrow again.

Buyer	: That's a good idea.
Maeng	: I hope we can close the deal tomorrow.
Buyer	: I hope so.
Maeng	: Thank you for your time. Let me give you a ride to the hotel.
Buyer	: Thanks.

Video 2-8

Maeng	: I'm so sorry that we couldn't make a deal.
Buyer	: I'm sorry, too. I hope we will have another opportunity to talk again in the future.
Maeng	: So do I. I'd like to express my deepest gratitude for your time and interest in our product.
Buyer	: You're very welcome.
Maeng	: Well, if you need any information or assistance, please don't hesitate to contact me. Thank you again. Good bye.
Buyer	: Thanks.

Video 2-9

Maeng	: Hello, may I help you?
Foreigner	: Yes. I'm looking for the Sam-Jung building.
Maeng	: Oh, I'm new around here, too. Why don't you ask the policeman over there?
Foreigner	: Oh, thank you so much.
Maeng	: You're welcome.

Video 2-10

Maeng	: Hello? May I help you?
Foreigner	: Yes, I'm lost.
Maeng	: What are you looking for?
Foreinger	: I'm looking for KBS.
Maeng	: Let me take a look at the map.
Foreigner	: Here you are.

Video 3-1

Maeng	: Hello, may I help you?

Foreinger : Yes, I want to go to Jong-Ro.

Maeng　　 : (There is no direct bus line to that place. you have to take bus No. 33 here, and get off at the City Hall stop, then take the subway line 1 there.) Oh, it's hard to get there by bus or subway.

I think you'd better take a taxi.

Video 3-2

Maeng　　 : Hello, are you lost?

Foreigner : Yes, I'm looking for the Yuk-Sam building.

Maeng　　 : Well, go straight ahead and turn left at the corner.

It's on the right-hand side at the end of the block.

You can't miss it.(It's easy to find it)

Foreigner : Oh, thank you so much.

Maeng　　 : You're welcome.

Video 3-3

Maeng　　 : Hello, can I recommend something to you?(Can I recommend a ride?)

Foreigner : Yes, please.

Maeng　　 : If I were you, I'd go to the Haunted House.(I'd take the Viking.)

It's really thrilling.

Foreigner : Oh, where is it?

Maeng　　 : It's right behind(in front of) the roller coaster. the roller coaster is on the left side of the Magic Kingdom. You can't miss it.

Foreigner : Thank you so much.

Maeng　　 : My pleasure.

Video 3-4

Foreigner : Excuse me, please. We're waiting in line here.(Don't cut the line.)

(=Don't be a breaker. First come, first served, you know.)

Maeng　　 : Oh, I'm sorry. I didn't know there was a line here.

Foreigner : Are you going to buy a ticket?

Maeng　　 : Yes, I'm going to(=gonna) buy a ticket for the roller coaster.

Foreigner : Well, you can save money by buying a one-day ticket(big 5).

Maeng　　 : Oh, I see. Thank you.

Foreigner : You're welcome.

Video 3-5

Park	: Good morning, Oliver.
Oliver	: Good morning, Mr. Park. How are you?
Park	: Fine thanks, and you?(I'm fine/not bad/so so/terrible)
Oliver	: Fine, Is that Mr. Maeng over there?
Park	: Yes, it is. Let me introduce you.
	Mr. Maeng. This is Oliver Piekarr.
Maeng	: how do you do?(How are you?)
Oliver	: Pleased(nice) to meet you, Mr. Maeng.
Maeng	: Please call me Maeng.
Oliver	: And please call me Oliver.

Video 3-6

Maeng	: I've worked for ABC Trading Company for five years.
Robert	: I'm from the head office of BPC. Nice to meet you.
Maeng	: Nice to meet you, too. I hope we have many opportunities to talk with each other.
Rovert	: I hope so, too.

Video 3-7

Larry	: Hi, Mr. Maeng.
Maeng	: Excuse me, but do I know you?
Larry	: We've met before.
Maeng	: I'm sorry. Where have we met?
Larry	: Robert Brown introduced me to you at your office. I'm Larry Smith.
Maeng	: Right, Mr. Smith! Now I remember. I'm very sorry I couldn't recognize you.
	I'm so forgetful.
Larry	: No problem.
Maeng	: How are things with you, Mr. Smith.
Larry	: Everything's fine.

Video 3-8

Larry	: Good morning, Mr. Maeng.
Maeng	: Good morning, Mr. Smith.
	I'd like you to meet Lee Yun-Kyoung.
Larry	: Hi, Miss Lee. How are you doing?
Miss Lee	: It's good to see you here.

Oliver	: Oh, you're Larry. I'm fine. How are you?
Larry	: I'm O.K.
Maeng	: How do you know each other? Have you met?
Larry	: We've met at your office before.
Maeng	: Really? It's a small world.

Video 3-9

Maeng	: Hello, John. Long time no see.
John	: Good morning, Maeng. I haven't seen you for a long time(=for ages).
Maeng	: where have you been hiding yourself? I've tried to get hold of you many times, but I couldn't get through.
John	: I've been on the road.
Maeng	: Quite busy, huh? You look prosperous, though.
John	: Thank you. You're looking good, too.

Video 3-10

Maeng	: Look who's here! If it isn't you, Larry?
Larry	: Hi, Mr. Maeng.
Maeng	: Fancy meeting you here. How are you doing?
Larry	: Just fine, thank you. How are you?
Maeng	: I'm fine. What brings you here?
Larry	: I have an appointment around here.
Maeng	: Oh, you're in a hurry. Keep in touch.
Larry	: O.K. Good-bye.
Maeng	: O.K. Good-bye.

Video 4-1

Larry	: I've heard about you through your manager. Would you tell me about your company?
Maeng	: Is there any product you're especially interested in?
Larry	: Nothing in particular. Just general goods.
Maeng	: We've specialized in general(electronic) goods for ten years.
Larry	: Is that right? Your company must have a good reputation.
Maeng	: I believe so.
Larry	: Thank you for the information.

Video 4-2

Laray	: Good afternoon, Mr. Maeng.(Practice makes perfect.)
Maeng	: Hi, Larry. I've been waiting for you.
Larry	: Oh, I'm sorry I'm late.
Maeng	: No problem. I know the traffic at this hour in Seoul.
	Step this way, please(=Come on: informal).
	I can't understand what you said.
	Is this your first visit to this kind of showroom?
Larry	: Yes. I always wanted to come but I never had the chance.
Maeng	: Good, I'll show you around Seoul.
Larry	: Thank you very much, Mr. Maeng.
Maeng	: My pleasure.(You're welcome.)

Video 4-3

Larry	: I enjoyed looking around.
	(May I help you? I'm just looking around.)
Maeng	: Was there any product(anything) you were especially(particularly) interested in?
Larry	: Well, I don't know. I'd have to think about it.
Maeng	: Right. If you need further information, please contact me.(Please get a hold of me.) Could I help you make your decision?
Larry	: Please do. Can I visit your factory?
Maeng	: Of course you can. Any time.
Larry	: I'd appreciate it(Oh, thank you), Mr. Maeng.
Maeng	: You're very welcome.

Video 4-4

Maeng	: You told you are good at tennis, right?
	Let's play tennis this Sunday. What do you say?(How about it?)
John	: Sunday is good. What time?
Maeng	: I like playing in the morning(How about some time in the morning?).
	It's too hot in the afternoon(later in the day).
	Would ten o'clock be okay?
John	: Fine. Where?
Maeng	: The tennis court behind my office.
John	: That would be good.
Maeng	: Okay, it's a date. See you on Sunday.

John   : Bye.

Video 4-5

John   : Hello. John Snieder.
Maeng   : Hello. David. This is Maeng. cf. You should never get too drunk.
John   : Good morning, Maeng. What can I do for you?
Maeng   : I'm calling you about our Sunday appointment.
            Something's come up suddenly.
John   : Oh, Would you like to change it then?
Maeng   : Would you mind?(Could I?) I'm free the day after tomorrow.
John   : Well, how about three o'clock in the afternoon?
Maeng   : Fine. I'm sorry to change things around like this.
John   : No problem.
Maeng   : See you then.
John   : all right. Bye.

Video 4-6

John   : Hello.
Maeng   : Hello, John. this is Maeng.
            I'm calling you about our Sunday appointment.
John   : What's wrong?(What's up?)
Maeng   : I'm sorry, but I'm afraid I can't make it myself.
            (I'm glad you could make it.)
            I have something to clear up in(at) my office.
John   : Is that so? Well, you can't help it.
Maeng   : But Mr. Kim will meet you.
John   : I wish I could see you.
Maeng   : I'm terribly(really) sorry, John. I'll get in touch with you later.
John   : Please do.

Video 4-7

Dave   : Hello.
            Maeng What's the matter, Dave? Why didn't you show up?
Dave   : That's what I was going to ask you.
            I waited for more than an hour.
Maeng   : Right. At five o'clock outside the palace.

Dave   : No. I was waiting inside the palace. Did you keep waiting outside?

Maeng   : Oh, no! We got the place mixed up!

Video 4-8

Dave   : You're late, Mr. Maeng.

          I've been waiting for more than thirty minutes.

Maeng   : I'm terribly sorry, david. I was tied up in traffic for over an hour.

          (I was tied up with work.)

          Actually it took me two hours to get here.

Dave   : Too bad. I understand.

Maeng   : i'm sorry again. Let me treat you to a nice dinner tonight.

Dave   : If you insist.

Video 4-9

Maeng   : Are you free in the morning on Thursday, Robert?

          (Are you available ....?)

Robert : No. I'm visiting a company in the morning How about the afternoon?

Maeng   : I'm afraid I can't make it then. How about Friday?

Robert : I'll be busy all day Friday.

          Would Saturday morning be good for you?

Maeng   : I'm sorry. I'm tied up Saturday morning.

          I'm free in the evening after eight o'clock.

Robert : That would be fine. What do you say to calling me at the hotel as soon as you're finished.

Maeng   : that would be good. Then I'll call you Saturday evening.

Robert : All right. I'll be waiting for your call.

Video 5-1

Maeng   : Dave, we're having(=holding) a party this Saturday.

          You have to come, of course.

Dave   : (Nice to hear from you.) That would be lovely.

          Thanks for inviting me.

Maeng   : Actually we're holding the party for you.

Dave   : Really? Thanks a lot. What time shall I come?

Maeng   : 7 : 00 in the evening. Will that suit you?(Will that be good for you?)

Dave   : Great. I'll see you then. Goodbye.

Maeng   : Bye. Thanks for inviting me to the party the other day.(Thank you again for
              your throwing the party for me the other day.)
              Now I'm inviting you to a party.(I'd like to invite you to a party.)

Video 5-2

Maeng   : David, what kind of party is it?

Dave   : Take a guess. Of course it's going to be a nice party.
              (Good guess!, Just a blind guess, Guess what.)
              Please come to the hotel, and I'll tell you then.

Maeng   : Okay, but is it a dress-up affair or a small get-together?

Dave   : Just casual.

Maeng   : All right. I'll see you at the hotel.

Video 5-3

Smith   : I was very happy about our meeting yesterday.

Maeng   : We were(I was) too, Mr. smith.

Smith   : Can I treat you to a drink tonight, Mr. Maeng?

Maeng   : Tonight? Let me check my calendar(schedule). I am sorry.
              I have a previous appointment. can I take a rain check, though?
              (Let's make it another time.)

Smith   : I'm sorry, too. Let's make it some other time.

Maeng   : Sorry.

Video 5-4

Smith   : Hi, Mr. Maeng.

Maeng   : Hi, Mr. Smith. (I'm) Sorry that I could not accept your invitation the other
              day. Please give me a chance to treat you to dinner tonight.

Smith   : I'll accept your offer.

Maeng   : You'll be surprised.

Smith   : About what?

Maeng   : There are many people I'd like to introduce you to.
              Anyway What time would you like me to pick you up?

Smith   : What time? Shall I say six o'clock?(Would 6 o'clock be o.k?/Would 6 o'clock
              be good for you?/Would 6 o'clock suit you?)

Maeng   : Six? Well, I wonder if I can make it. How about seven?

Smith   : No problem.

Maeng   : Good.

Video 5-5 (In front of the hotel)

Maeng   : I'm (over)here. Hop in, please.

Smith   : Thank you. It took too much time to get here.
            Have we arrived on time?

Maeng   : Right on the dot. Everybody's (already) arrived I believe. Please hurry.(Lets
            get in there./ Let's hurry.)

Video 5-6

Maeng   : I hope you enjoyed yourself, Mr. Smith.(I hope you had a good time.)

Smith   : Absolutely. I had great fun.(I certainly did.)
            And I met a lot of nice people, thanks to you.

Maeng   : I hope it's going to be a good memory of your stay in Korea.
            Can I give you a lift(=ride) to the hotel?

Smith   : No, thanks. I've already given you too much trouble.
            I can(will) take a taxi here.

Maeng   : Come on! It is the least I can do.

Video 5-7

Maeng   : Would you like to do some shopping?

David   : Yes, I'm interested in something typically Korean.
            Something small, I think.

Maeng   : Is that right? Then we'd better go to a souvenir shop. Let me see...
            Where should we go? Ah, I've just remembered a nice place.
            (=Now I remember a nice place.)

Cavid   : Is it far from here?

Maeng   : Sort of, but I'm afraid it's too late for today.

David   : Good. Thank you.

Maeng   : You're very welcome.

Video 5-8

Maeng   : Here we are.

David   : Quit a variety! This one is real cute. What is it?
            (cf. He's a quit a guy.)

Maeng   : Well, it's called dolharubang in Korean.

It's produced on Cheju Island. It's part of shamanism.

David   : I see. What about this toy? Is it also part of shamanism?

Maeng   : No, it's not. It's Tal in Korean, a traditional mask. People, especially farmers, used to get together and dance wearing Tals.

Video 5-9 (In a Korean restaurant)

David   : So this is a Korean restaurant?

Maeng   : Right. I think You'll like this place. (After being served) This is the most representative Korean food. It's called Kimchi in Korean.

Why don't you try it?

David   : yes. My God! It's too hot!

Maeng   : It's flavored with ground red pepper.

David   : What's this?

Maeng   : Bulgogi, a Korean's favorite. Sort of grilled beef.

David   : (After trying) Boy! This is delicious!

Maeng   : I told you, didn't I?

Video 6-1

Maeng   : Hey, Robert! Wait. According to our table manners, you should start eating after the older people do.

Robert   : I'm sorry. I didn't know that. Mr. Maeng, I have a question.

Maeng   : What is it? Go ahead.

Robert   : Why are there so many dishes only for one course(round) of dinner?

Maeng   : We usually prepare a wide variety of foods for guests.

That's our custom. cf. Fix dinner.(o). Fix foods(x)

Robert   : I see.

Video 6-2

Robert   : Mr. Maeng. How much is this(one of these/ a set)?

Maeng   : About three dollars.

Robert   : Oh, it's too expensive. Could he give me a discount?(Could you give it to me at a lower price? /Could you come down a little more?)

Maeng   : He says this is the best he can do (for you).

Robert   : Please get him come down a little.

Maeng	: Okay, I'll try. (But) I'm not sure.
Robert	: thank you, Mr. Maeng.

Video 6-3

Robert	: Where is this?
Maeng	: This is Kyongbok Gung(Palace), the biggest palace in Korea. Built in theYi Dynasty, this is one of the most famous tourist attractions in Korea.
Robert	: Beautiful! just fantastic!
Maeng	: Not only foreign tourists but also a lot of Korean holiday makers visit this palace on weekends.
Robert	: Oh, I see. I'm quit lucky to come here during this trip.

Video 6-4

Maeng	: Hey, Dave! Let me take a picture of you. This is a nice place for taking pictures, (isn't it?)
Dave	: Yes, it is.
Maeng	: Okay. Stand up, please. Say "cheese" (laughing) "kimchi" is better. Good.
Dave	: Now it's your turn. Stand over there under the tree.
Maeng	: No thanks, Dave. I'm camera-shy.

Video 6-5

Maeng	: There's another thing you should know about our table manners.
Dave	: What is it?
Maeng	: Even if you've finished the meal, you should not leave the table unless you are excused by older people.
Dave	: I see. You know what, Maeng? I feel very uncomfortable with chopsticks. Can I ask for a fork?
Maeng	: Oh, anytime. Do you want a fork now?
Dave	: Yes, please.
Maeng	: Don't worry. I'll ask for one for you.

Video 6-6

Maeng	: Hey, David. How about this (one)?
David	: It's nice. How much is it? (Oh, that looks good on you./Oh, that suit you.)
Maeng	: About 15 dollars.

Dave   : Oh, it's too expensive, but I like it.

             Please ask her to give me a discount.

Maeng : She said it's the rock-bottom(top) price.(The price is already fixed.)

Dave   : Okay, I'll take it.

Maeng : I think it's(that's) a good deal.

Video 6-7

Dave   : This is a much bigger place than I thought.

Maeng : Yes. This restaurant is noted for traditional Korean foods.

             They say Galbee is extra-good here.

Dave   : I can't tell what's what.

Maeng : That's not your fault. You'd better follow my example.

Dave   : Very good. I'll have the same as you. I'm in your hands.

Video 6-8

Maeng : I can't stand waiting around!

Dave   : Do you come here often?

Maeng : This is the second time.

Dave   : Ah, here it comes at last! Better late than never!

Maeng : Now I come to think of it, it was the same the last time I was here.

             I'd better steer clear of this place next time.

Video 6-9

Maeng : Have some more, please.

Dave   : Oh, no. this is enough.

Maeng : Gosh, you eat like a bird.

Dave   : Not at all. I'm just not a big eater.

Maeng : Let me give you some vegetables.

Dave   : Only very little, please. Oh, less than that!

Maeng : It's only a small helping.

Dave   : It's plenty, thank you.

Video 7-1

Maeng : There's nothing like a cigarette after dinner.

Dave   : I understand because I used to smoke a lot, too.

Maeng	: You don't smoke at all now? How did you manage to quit?
Dave	: Actually, I often quit for weeks at a time, but I started again and again.
Maeng	: Then how did you do it(=quit smoking)?
Dave	: One day I made up my mind and gave it up altogether.
Maeng	: Right. I heard going(=quitting) cold turkey is the best way to quit smoking.

Video 7-2

Maeng	: What do you think about him?
Dave	: Well, he seems to be a very matter-of -fact sort of guy- at least that's the impression he gave me. What's he like?
Maeng	: That's what he is. No emotion. No imagination.
Dave	: He's not popular at all, is he?
Maeng	: He is, though. Well, there's no accounting for tastes. (Beauty lies in the eye of the beholder. One man's meat is other man's poison.)
Dave	: You're absolutely right.

Video 7-3

Maeng	: Is this book up your alley?
Dave	: I say, it's real funny!
Maeng	: Is it a novel?
Dave	: It's Neil Simon's - Barefoot in the Park.
Maeng	: Is that the book? It's one I've been waiting to read for a long time. Where did you get hold of it?
Dave	: Oh, I picked it up second-hand bookstore in Chicago. I'll give it to you after I read it.
Maeng	: I'd appreciate it, Dave.

Video 7-4

Maeng	: What are you planning to do this weekend?
Dave	: I don't know. Maybe i'm going to read a couple of books.
Maeng	: What(It's) a shame to stay indoors on the weekend! Let's go on a trip together. What do you say?
Dave	: Well.... I hate the traffic.
Maeng	: Come on, Dave! You won't regret. I promise.
Dave	: Where we going?

Maeng   : There's a nice place I had in mind. But we can find another place if you like. let's look at the map.

Video 7-5

Maeng   : (Pointing to the map) This is the place I wanted to go to.
Dave   : I'm afraid it's too far from here.
Maeng   : Not at all. It will take about five hours. If we leave Saturday afternoon, we can come back Sunday evening.
Dave   : You've got to work Monday morning.
Maeng   : You're right. How about Songdo? It's not so far, and it's a nice place, too.
Dave   : Let's give it some more thought.

Video 7-6

Dave   : Okay, let's go to the place you had in mind.
Maeng   : It's a date, right?
Dave   : Yes, it is. By the way, how are we getting(going) there? Will we take the express bus?
Maeng   : I don't think so. We'd better take the train. Saemaeul is the fastest one. You'll feel very comfortable.
Dave   : I like the train.
Maeng   : Me, too.

Video 7-7

Maeng   : Hey, David. So sorry to keep you waiting. I took the wrong train by mistake. Nuts!
Dave   : That's all right. The weather is just beautiful. It's brought all the people out.
Maeng   : Yeah, Splendid.
Dave   : I hope it'll hold.
Maeng   : No doubt about it. We're going on a trip.
Dave   : You got that right! Let's get going.

Video 7-8

Dave   : What's wrong?
Maeng   : The engine won't start.
Dave   : Don't hold the accelerator down! You'll flood the engine.

Maeng : You are right.

Dave : You'd better turn off the ignition(=engine) and wait a minute or two.
Then try it again.(turn off the engine ≠ start / ignite the engine)

Maeng : (In a couple of minutes) It doesn't work.

Dave : We ought to push it over toward the curb.

Video 8-1

Maeng : How did you like the trip?

Dave : It was just great.

Maeng : Don't you think you should have stayed at home and read those books?

Dave : What are you talking about? I really enjoyed myself....though I still can't
forget the terrible traffic getting there.

Maeng : I know. Anyhow I'm pleased to hear that you had fun.

Dave : Thanks for everything, Maeng.

Maeng : You're very welcome.

Video 8-2

Maeng : David, I want to study English systematically.

Dave : Why don't you study in a private institute?

Maeng : What do you think about making a club in the company?

Dave : An English conversation club?

Maeng : Yes, I think it's good for fellowship, too. I mean, We can kill two birds with one stone.

Dave : That's a good idea, Maeng. I'd be willing to help you.

Video 8-3

Dave : Maeng, how is it coming along? The club?

Maeng : Not good. It's very slow.

Dave : What's the problem?

Maeng : Busy! Busy! Busy! Why are they so busy after work?

Dave : I'm afraid they're just making excuses.

Maeng : I know they have enough time. They just chicken out.

Dave : What a let-down!

Maeng : Dave, cheer up. I'll start the club one way or another.

Video 8-4

David : Hi, Maeng.

Maeng	: Hi, David.
	I have a good news for you, Dave. Mr. Kim and Miss Lee decided to join the club.
Dave	: Really? That's great!
Maeng	: Now I've got to buckle down.
	"Well begun is half done," as they say.
Dave	: I'm sure it's going to be successful.
Maeng	: Of course. Let's drink to that tonight.
Dave	: That sounds good, Maeng.

Video 8-5

Maeng	: Now we've got to register our club.
Dave	: How?
Maeng	: Let me check in the regulations. Let me see.... first of all, We receive an application form, fill it out, and submit it to the General Affairs Department.
Dave	: It's quit easy.
Maeng	: Yes. but.... it's not approved unless there are more than five members.
Dave	: We only have four! (Right at the moment the section chief says he's going to join.)

Video 8-6

Dave	: Now let us listen to Mr. Maeng who has played a major role in making this club. Let's give him a big hand. (Applause)
Maeng	: Thank you all. I'm Maeng, a chief clerk. I'm really happy to be with you today. I feel like I'm a father of a new baby.
	As you may probably know, I'm very poor in English. But There are many people who wish to speak English well, and I'm on the top of the list. Of course you do, too, I believe. I hope all the members here will be able to converse in English very well as quickly as possible. Thank you again, and good luck.

Video 8-7

Robert	: Hi, I'm Robert.
Maeng	: I'm Maeng. Glad to meet you.
	Where did you work before?
Robert	: I worked in the head office of BPC for five years.
Maeng	: Is that right? Then you must be an expert at trading.
	Well, this department is always loaded down with work.
	You've got to brace yourself for hard work, I'm afraid.

Robert : I've heard about that, and actually I'm ready for it.

Video 8-8

Robert : This is the list of things I've prepared.
Would you please look at it?

Maeng : Oh, sure. This is incredible! You did a very good job.
It must have taken lots of time to complete.

Robert : I did, but I'm very pleased you like it.

Maeng : You deserve high praise for this.

Robert : Thank you. I take that as a compliment.

Video 8-9

Maeng : Robert, could you do me a favor?

Robert : Sure. What is it?

Maeng : Have a seat. I've got to work overtime tonight, and I need your help.

Robert : What can I do for you?

Maeng : I write poorly in English.
I must submit this essay by tomorrow morning.
Can you proofread it for me?

Robert : Okay, no problem.

Maeng : Thank you very much, Robert.

Video 9-1

Robert : Maeng, could you give me a ride to my apartment after work?

Maeng : Gee, I'm sorry, Robert. I have an appointment.

Robert : It's an important appointment, I guess.

Maeng : Well, actually it's a date. Really important to me.

Robert : No doubt. Then never mind, Maeng.

Maeng : I'm sorry again, Robert.

Video 9-2

Maeng : Robert, what's taking so long?
I've been waiting for your report.

Robert : I'm sorry, I've been awfully busy with something else.

Maeng : Do you know what your trouble is?

You often get your priorities switched!

Robert : I'm really sorry. I'll finish it as quickly as possible.

Maeng : Please do, and don't let it happen again.

Robert : I see.

Video 9-3

Robert : Cid you go o9ver my proposal?

Maeng : Oh I did. Let me see. It's very good.

It was accepted with unanimous approval.

Robert : I'm pleased to hear that.

Maeng : The chief liked it very much.

Now you can start designing the details for it.

Robert : Yes, I will.

Maeng : Please don't hesitate to propose your ideas any time.

Video 9-4

Robert : What do you think of my proposal?

Maeng : Well, your idea is really good, but.... I mean.

It's basically good, but I'm wondering if it's possible to put it into effect.

Robert : Nothing's a hundred percent definite at the beginning.

No venture, no gain, I believe.

Maeng : I agree, but still we'd better think it over again before we put it forward for approval.

Video 9-5

Dave : Why didn't you tell me there was a phone call for me from the BPC head office?

Maeng : Oh, nuts! I just forgot it! I'm really sorry, Dave.

Dave : A lot of good being sorry does.

That was a very important call, you know.

Maeng : I don't know how to apologize to you.

What's going to happen?

Dave : Well, I don't know.

I think I have to contact someone in the office.

Video 9-6

Dave : Maeng, you were too sensitive(≠generous).

It was nothing to yell about.

Maeng : I couldn't stand it. They picked the fight.

Dave : We must make this deal a success, you know.

Maeng : Trust me. I'll attend to the contract all right.

There must be a way.

Dave : Your personality!

Maeng : I know I'm thin-skinned(hot-blooded); That's part of my nature, though.

Video 9-7

Dave : Maeng, we're in big trouble now. There's a claim on our goods we shipped to Taiwan last month.

Maeng : What? A claim on our shipment?

How could that happen? Now what?

Dave : Come down(cool it/take it easy), Maeng.

Maeng : Okay, I'm all right.

The claim was on the whole shipment?

Dave : No, not the whole shipment. 20% or so.

Maeng : It's consoling to hear that.

I think we've got to report it to the chief right away.

Video 9-8

Maeng : Dave, I was dead drunk last night, wasn't I?

Did I make any mistakes?

Dave : Don't you remember anything?

Don't you remember we went to Cats for the third round?

Maeng : I do, but I can't remember what happened there.

I'm afraid I was too drunk there.

Dave : Shame on you last night! You yelled in the street!

Maeng : I'm sorry, Dave. I've got to control how much I drink next time.

Video 9-9

Maeng : Dave, did you use my fountain pen?

Dave : Yes, but.... eh.... I.... I can't find it anywhere.

Maeng : What Did you lost it? Oh no!

You know I treasure it, don't you?

How could you lost it?

Dave	: You're too hard on me, Meang. It's just a fountain pen.
Maent	: Just a fountain pen?
	It was a present my professor gave me in commemoration of my graduation.
Dave	: I didn't know that. I'm very sorry, Maeng.

Video 9-10

Maeng	: Good morning, David. This is Maeng.
	I'd rather not to work today.
Dave	: Why? What's the matter?
Maeng	: I don't feel well. I'm afraid I'm coming down with a cold.
	Would you call the chief for me, please?
	And tell him I've developed a bad cold, so I can't come to work today.
Dave	: Don't worry. He'll say you should stay in bed.
	Take care.

Video 10-1

Dave	: Say, Maeng, You had a call from an insurance man just a minute ago, and you're supposed to call him back.
Maeng	: An insurance man! Oh, gosh no!
Dave	: What's the matter with that?
Maeng	: He really drives me out of my mind! I'm sure glad you didn't give him my home phone number.
Dave	: Oh, but I did!
Maeng	: My God!

- I sold ten fire insurance policies last week.
  - 난 지난주에 화재보험 10건 팔았다.
- I bought a life insurance policy. - 난 생명보험에 들었다.

Video 10-2

Maeng	: Oh! Did you see What I just did?
Dave	: See what?
Maeng	: I just spilled my coffee on your jacket.
	Let me get something to clean it up.
Dave	: That's all right. I'll get it.
Maeng	: Gee, I'm sure sorry about that!

I hope I didn't ruin it.

Looks like it's a brand new one.

Dave   : It'll be all right. No problem.

- I'm so(sure, terribly, awfully) sorry. - 매우 미안하다.
- That's OK. = No problem. - 괜찮아요.

Video 10-3

Maeng   : Did you finish the book I lent you?

Dave   : Well, you see... I...

Maeng   : What's the matter, david? Something wrong?

Dave   : I'm sorry, Maeng. I... lost it.

Maeng   : You what?

Dave   : Well, can you forgive me?

Maeng   : Dave, you lost my book? My favorite book!

How could you do that!

Dave   : Well, please forgive me.

- Did you finish the book? - 그 책 다 읽었니?
- Which school did you finish? - 어느 학교를 졸업했니?

Video 10-4

Dave   : Maeng, I have some news for you.

Maeng   : Good or bad?

Dave   : Take a guess.

Maeng   : I hope it's good news.

Dave   : Yes! We got the contract with the ABS Company!

Maeng   : Boy, oh boy! Isn't that great!

Drinks on me tonight!

- Get a contract = win(secure) a contract - 계약을 따내다.
- Drinks on me = I'll buy you a drink. - 내가 한잔 사지.

Video 10-5

Maeng   : What's the matter with you, Dave?

You look worried.

Dave   : Do I? There's a reason.

Maeng   : What's that?

Dave   : John lost his job.

Maeng   : Oh, did he? Gee, that's too bad.

Dave   : Yeah, the company wasn't making enough money, so they had to lay off some employees.

Maeng   : I'm really sorry to hear that!

- Lay off = fire - 해고하다.

Video 10-6

Dave   : Did you have fun at the party? Nice people, eh?

Maeng   : No doubt about it. But I still feel shamed.

I'm a disgrace to my family.

Dave   : What? Why do you feel like that?

Maeng   : You know how terrible my English was when I talked with your friends, and after more than ten years of studying it since I was in middle school and high school! I am so stupid!

Dave   : Cheer up, Maeng. Your English is good enough.

You're speaking correct English now, aren't you?

Maeng   : Thank you for saying so.

- I feel shamed. - 스스로 창피하다고 느끼다.
- Shame on you. - 자네 창피한 줄 알게나.
- It's so stupid of you to say so. - 어찌 그리 어처구니없는 말을 하니.

Video 10-7

Dave   : Guess what! I just got invited to Mr. Hong's house for dinner. He's moved into a new house quite recently.

Maeng   : That's great, but do you know what you do when you're invited to a housewarming party in Korea?

Dave   : That I don't know. That's why I'm telling you about it.

Maeng   : Oh, you usually bring a box of detergent or a big box of matches to wish prosperity for the household.

Dave   : I didn't know that. Thanks for the advice.

- Move into = move out of - 이사하다.
- Housewarming party - 집들이
- To wish prosperity - 번영을 기원하다.

Video 10-8

Dave   : What's the shortest way to the Trade Center from here? The Olympic Freeway?

Maeng	: Are you driving?
Dave	: Yes.
Maeng	: I'd take Taehaeran Ro, if I were you.
	There's too much traffic on the freeway at this hour.
Dave	: You're right. Thank you, Maeng.
Maeng	: My pleasure.

- Highway=express way - 고속도로
- Freeway - 통행료가 없는 도로
- There's too much traffic. - 교통이 매우 혼잡하다.

Video 10-9

Maeng	: Dave, do you know what John's going to do now that he lost his job?
Dave	: Well, I don't know. Maybe he's thinking of starting his own business. I don't know what I'd do if I lost my job. Maybe I'd go back to school. What would you do?
Maeng	: Me? Well, first I think I'd probably take a vacation. After that, I guess I'd try working for myself, too. I don't think I'd ever go back to school!

- Do one's own business = Work for oneself
  (개인 사업을 하다.)
- Do business with~ - 누구와 거래를 하다.

Video 10-10

Dave	: Are you going with us to the baseball game?
Maeng	: Maybe, I'm not sure.
Dave	: You'd better make up your mind. We're leaving in a few minutes.
Maeng	: I've got a lot of things to do this afternoon. Besides, I'm not really sure I want to go to the game. You go ahead. I'm going to stay here.
Dave	: What a shame!

- I'm not sure. = I don't know for sure. - 확신하지 못한다.
- It depends. - 상황에 따라서 변할 가능성이 있다.

3. *Phonological changes*(음운 변화)

소리의 변화 규칙과 발음원리를 이해해야 귀가 뚫리고 입이 열린다.

발음규칙 1

[t]는 모음 사이에서 [r]로 소리난다

[강모음 + t + 약모음]

자음 [t]가 강모음과 약모음 사이에 오면 여린 [t] ⇨ [r]음에 가깝게 발음된다. 우리말의 [ㄹ]에 가깝게 들린다.

WORD PRONUNCIATION PRACTICE

• water	[워터]	[워-러ㄹ]
• better	[베터]	[베-러ㄹ]
• hospital	[호스피틀]	[하-스삐러-ㄹ]
• Peter	[피터]	[피-러ㄹ]
• automatic	[오토매틱]	[아-로매-릭]
• computer	[컴퓨터]	[컴퓨-러ㄹ]
• matter	[매터]	[매-러ㄹ]
• bottom	[보톰]	[바-럼]
• sitting	[씨팅]	[씨링] [씨-린]
• meeting	[미팅]	[미링] [미-린]
• located	[로케이티드]	[(을)로 케이-리드]
• United States	[유나이티드 스테이츠]	[유 나-이리드 스떼-이츠]

SENTENCE PRONUNCIATION PRACTICE

1. Please give me some **water** to drink.
2. You'd **better** go to the **hospital**, **Peter**.
3. Is your car a stick shift?   No, it's an **automatic**.
4. When did you buy the **computer**?   I bought it last year.
5. What's the **matter** with you?   Nothing.
6. There are a lot of fish at the **bottom** of the sea.
7. The old woman **sitting** in the chair is my grandmother.
8. Because of a traffic jam, I was late for the **meeting**.
9. My school is **located** in Shinlim Dong.
10. Jimmy Carter is a former president of the **United States**.

〈참고〉 drink : 규칙 8   You'd : 규칙 25   is your : 규칙 23   did you : 규칙 7   what's the : 규칙 16   lot of : 규칙 1
Carter : 규칙 3

발음규칙 2

[d]도 모음 사이에서 [r]로 소리난다

[강모음 + d + 약모음]

자음 [d]가 강모음과 약모음 사이에 오면 여린 [d] ⇨ [r]에 가깝게 발음된다. 우리말의 [ㄹ]에 가까운 소리가 난다.

WORD PRONUNCIATION PRACTICE

• everybody	[에브리보디]	[에-ㅂ흐리바리]
• daddy	[대디]	[대-리]
• lady	[레이디]	[(을)레-이리]
• modern	[모던]	[마-런]
• model	[모델]	[마-러-ㄹ]
• medal	[메달]	[메-러-ㄹ]
• already	[올레디]	[오-ㄹ(우)레-리]
• cloudy	[클라우디]	[클 라-우리]
• video game	[비디오 게임]	[ㅂ희-리오 게-임]
• credit card	[크레딧 카드]	[크레-릿 카ㄹ드]

SENTENCE PRONUNCIATION PRACTICE

1. Good morning, **everybody**.
2. Can you give me a ride to school, **daddy**?
3. Who's that **lady**?
4. It is important to know how to dance in **modern** society.
5. I'm making a **model** airplane now.
6. I won a gold **medal** at the 88 Seoul Olympic Games.
7. I've **already** finished the work.
8. It's **cloudy**. It'll clear up soon.
9. I enjoyed a **video game** last night.
10. I lost my **credit card** in the bus.

〈참고〉 society : 규칙 1 I'm, I've, It'll : 규칙 25 making : 규칙 20 won a, clear up : 규칙 13 last night : 규칙 5
in the : 규칙 16

발음규칙 3

[rt]도 모음 사이에서 [r]로 소리난다
[강모음 + rt + 약모음]

자음 [rt]나 [rd]가 강모음과 약모음 사이에 오면 [rt]나 [rd]는
⇨ [r]로 발음된다. 우리말의 [ㄹ]에 가깝게 소리 난다.

WORD PRONUNCIATION PRACTICE

• dirty	[더티]	[더-ㄹ리]
• portable	[포터블]	[포-ㄹ러브-ㄹ]
• party	[파티]	[파-ㄹ리]
• reporter	[리포터]	[리포-ㄹ러ㄹ]
• shorter	[쇼터]	[쇼-ㄹ러ㄹ]
• thirty	[써티]	[ㅎ떠-ㄹ리]
• comfortable	[컴훠터블]	[캄-ㅍ훠러브-ㄹ]
• article	[아티클]	[아르-러크-ㄹ]
• harder	[하더]	[하ㄹ-러ㄹ]
• where do you	[웨어 두 유]	[웨-어 류]

SENTENCE PRONUNCIATION PRACTICE

1. Your room is **dirty**. Please clean the room right now.
2. I want to buy a **portable** stereo.
3. Thank you very much for coming to my birthday **party**.
4. I want to be a **reporter** after I graduate.
5. Tom is **shorter** than my brother.
6. Do you have the time?　　　　　It's seven **thirty**.
7. How do you like the apartment?　　I think it's **comfortable**.
8. The **article** she reported yesterday was great.
9. You have to study English much **harder**.
10. **Where do you** live now?

〈참고〉 clean the, than : 규칙 16　　Thank you : 규칙 15　　graduate, do you : 규칙 7　　shorter than : 규칙 16
apartment : 규칙 3, 5　reported : 규칙 3

발음규칙 4

[nt], [nd]는 모음 사이에서 [n]으로 소리난다
[강모음 + nt + 약모음]

자음 [nt]나 [nd] 앞에 강모음이 오고, 뒤에 약모음이 오면
[nt], [nd] ⇨ [n]으로 발음된다. 이 때 t음과 d음이 n음에 동화
되어 t와 d가 생략된다.

WORD PRONUNCIATION PRACTICE

• center	[쎈터]	[쎄-너ㄹ]
• dentist	[덴티스트]	[데-니스ㅌ]
• international	[인터내셔널]	[이너ㄹ내-셔너-ㄹ]
• interview	[인터뷰]	[이-너ㄹㅂ휴]
• counter	[카운터]	[카-우너ㄹ]
• Toronto	[토론토]	[투(우)라-노]
• wanted	[원티드]	[워-니ㄷ]
• painting	[페인팅]	[페-이닌]
• printed	[프린티드]	[프(우)리-니ㄷ]
• understand	[언더스텐드]	[언더ㄹ스땐-ㄷ]
• round	[라운드]	[(우)라-운ㄷ]

SENTENCE PRONUNCIATION PRACTICE

1. There used to be a big fountain in the **center** of the square.
2. I have a toothache. Why don't you go see a **dentist**?
3. I think English is the **international** language.
4. When I was at an **interview**, I was very nervous in fron of the examiner.
5. There are lots of people around the **counter** in the supermarket all the time.
6. I didn't fly to **Toronto** last week because I couldn't get a plane ticket.
7. I **wanted** to start **painting** just as a hobby.
8. A lot of books were **printed** in Korea in 1995.
9. can't **understand** what you said.
10. That mountain is covered with white snow all the year **round**.

〈참고〉 used to : 규칙 27 square : 규칙 10 don't you, what you : 규칙 7 at an, get a : 규칙 1 all the : 규칙 16

발음규칙 5

[t]는 자음 사이나 자음 뒤에서 탈락된다
[자음 + t + 자음]

자음 사이에 오는 [t]음은 탈락되는 경향이 많다.
[nt]음에서 [t]음이 보통 생략된다.

WORD PRONUNCIATION PRACTICE

• just now	[죠스트 나우]	[져-스 나우]
• last weekend	[라스트 윅엔드]	[(을)래-스 윅껜]
• next week	[넥스트 위크]	[넥-스 윅]
• must be	[머스트 비]	[머-스 비]
• best friend	[베스트 후렌드]	[베-스 프후렌]
• isn't	[이즌트]	[이-즌ㅌ]
• don't	[돈트]	[도-운ㅌ]
• doesn't	[더즌트]	[더-즌ㅌ]
• can't	[캔트]	[캐-엔]
• haven't	[해븐트]	[해-ㅂ흔]

SENTENCE PRONUNCIATION PRACTICE

1. I finished writing my report **just now**.
2. Why so blue? Jane stood me up **last weekend**.
3. I'm going to leave New York **next week**.
4. You **must be** honest and sincere wherever you work.
5. My **best friend** has gone to Brazil. I miss him.
6. This chair **isn't** comfortable for me.
7. I **don't** know how to thank you enough.
8. It **doesn't** matter. **Don't** worry about it.
9. **can't** remember what I did last night.
10. I **haven't** got any money to buy that bag.

〈참고〉 writing : 규칙 1 stood me : 규칙 6 going to : 규칙 27 comfortable : 규칙 3 thank you : 규칙 15 about it, what I : 규칙 1

발음규칙 6

[d]도 자음 사이나 자음 뒤에서 탈락된다
[자음 + d + 자음]

자음 사이에 오는 [d]음은 탈락되는 경향이 있다. 특히 l이나 n 뒤에서는 [d]음이 생략되고 생략된 음의 길이만큼 끌어 준다.

WORD PRONUNCIATION PRACTICE

• old man	[올드 맨]	[오-(을)ㄷ 맨]
• cold night	[콜드 나이트]	[코-(을)ㄷ 나-잇]
• old fashioned	[올드 훼숀드]	[오-(을)ㄷ ㅍ훼-션]
• told me	[토울드 미]	[토-(을) 미]
• world news	[월드 뉴스]	[워ㄹ-(을)ㄷ 누스]
• weekend	[위크엔드]	[윜-껜ㄷ]
• Would you mind checking	[우드 유 마인드 체킹]	[우쥬 마인 첵낀]
• round trip ticket	[라운드 트립 티켓]	[(우)라운 츄립 티킷]
• beyond my ability	[비요인드 마이 어빌리티]	[비요인 마이 어빌-러리]
• understand me	[언덜스텐드 미]	[언더ㄹ 스땐 미]

SENTENCE PRONUNCIATION PRACTICE

1. It's dangerous for an **old man** to climb a mountain covered with snow.
2. I saw a girl walking along the street one **cold night**.
3. The dress you bought the other day is **old fashioned**.
4. He **told me** that he got a new job last month.
5. I was surprised to read the article in the **world news**.
6. Have a nice **weekend**.   Same to you.
7. **Would you mind checking** my report?   Not at all.
8. A **round trip ticket** is usually cheaper than two one way tickets.
9. Your request is **beyond my ability**.
10. You mean you can **understand me**?

〈참고〉 walking : 규칙 20   street : 규칙 8   got a, Not at : 규칙 1   last month : 규칙 5   article : 규칙 3   cheaper than : 규칙 16

발음규칙 7 | [d, t] 뒤에 [j]가 오면 [dʒ, tʃ]로 소리난다
[d, t + j]

한 단어와 단어 사이에서 [d]나 [t] 뒤에 반모음 [j]가 오면 [d, d, + j ⇨ dʒ], [t, tʃ + j ⇨ tʃ]로 바뀐다. 이처럼 자음과 반모음이 만나 다른 음으로 변한다.

WORD PRONUNCIATION PRACTICE

• individual	[인디ㅂ흐듀얼]	[인디 ㅂ휘-주어-ㄹ]
• schedule	[스케듈]	[스 께-쥬-ㄹ]
• could you	[쿠드 유]	[쿠 쥬]
• would you	[우드 유]	[우 쥬]
• did you	[디드 유]	[디 쥬]
• natural	[내튜럴]	[내-츄러-ㄹ]
• don't you	[돈트 유]	[돈 츄], [돈 유]
• didn't you	[디든트 유]	[디든 츄]
• get your	[겟 유어]	[겟 츄어ㄹ]
• what you	[윗 유]	[윗 츄]

SENTENCE PRONUNCIATION PRACTICE

1. Could you cut this cake into **individual** servings?
2. I'm sorry, but I have a heavy **schedule** tonight.
3. **Could you** give me some cold water?
4. **Would you** like to join us for dinner tonight?
5. **Did you** figure out how to get there?
6. It is **natural** that you should relax your mind after all that studying.
7. Why **don't you** leave your name?
8. Why **didn't you** attend the meeting yesterday?
9. How can I **get your** friend back home?
10. I can't understand **what you** are saying.

〈참고〉 cake : 규칙 10   but I : 규칙 1   have a, join us, figure out, leave your, can I : 규칙 13   mind : 규칙 4
attend : 규칙 4   meeting : 규칙 20, 1

발음규칙 8

[dr, tr] 뒤에 모음이 오면 [dʒr, tʃr]로 소리난다

[dr, tr + 모음]

[dr, tr] 뒤에 모음이 오면 dr ⇨ [dʒr], tr ⇨ tʃr]이 된다. 우리 말의 [쥬]와 [츄]로 발음된다.

WORD PRONUNCIATION PRACTICE

• drawer	[드로워]	[쥬로-워ㄹ]
• drink	[드링크]	[쥬링-ㅋ]
• dream	[드림]	[쥬리-ㅁ]
• drive	[드라이브]	[쥬라-이ㅂ흐]
• dress	[드레스]	[쥬레-스]
• train	[트레인]	[츄레-인]
• tree	[트리]	[츄리-]
• trip	[트립]	[츄립]
• trouble	[투러블]	[츄라-브-ㄹ]
• traffic	[트래ㅍ휙]	[츄래-ㅍ휙]

SENTENCE PRONUNCIATION PRACTICE

1. Where are my socks?   They're in the **drawer**.
2. How about passing around **drinks**?
3. My **dream** is to go on a trip all over the world.
4. Can you **drive** me to school this morning, daddy?
5. She didn't **dress** properly for the interview.
6. I got up early in the morning to catch the first **train**.
7. I found Christmas presents under the Christmas **tree**.
8. My hobby is going on a **trip** and taking pictures.
9. Is it **true** that his son became a **trouble** maker?
10. Because of a heavy **traffic**, I was thirty minutes late for the meeting.

〈참고〉 in the : 규칙 16 around drink : 규칙 6 on a trip : 규칙 13, 8 interview : 규칙 4 got up : 규칙 1 first train : 규칙 3 thirty : 규칙 3 minutes : 규칙 29

발음규칙
9

[dl, tl, dn, tn] 사이에 "―"대신 "ㅅ"을 넣어 소리낸다

[d, t, n] + l, n]

강음절 뒤에 오는 [dl], [tl], [dn], [tn] 등은 [d], [t]와 [l], [n] 사이에 불필요한 [―]모음을 발음하지 않고 [ㅅ] 받침을 붙여 발음하고 [ㅅ]에서 숨을 멈췄다가 소리낸다.

WORD PRONUNCIATION PRACTICE

• hardly	[하―드리]	[하―ㄹ을리]
• brightly	[브라이트리]	[브라―잇을리]
• lately	[레이트리]	[(을)레―잇을리]
• certainly	[썰튼리]	[써ㄹㅅ은(을)리]
• kindly	[카인드리]	[카―인을리]
• all of a sudden	[올 오브 어 써든]	[올―러ㅂ허 써ㅅ은]
• garden	[갈든]	[가―ㄹㅅ은]
• written	[리튼]	[(우)리ㅅ은]
• mountain	[마운튼]	[마―운ㅅ은]
• Newton	[뉴턴]	[뉴―ㅅ은]

SENTENCE PRONUNCIATION PRACTICE

1. I can **hardly** hear you.   We seem to have a bad connection.
2. Smiling **brightly**, she came up to me.
3. How have you been **lately**?   I.m fine.
4. Could you do me a favor?   **Certainly**.
5. He **kindly** solved my problem.
6. **All of a sudden** the windows and cups on the table were shaken.
7. I saw trees covered with white snow in the **garden**.
8. The fictions **written** by Mr. Park were very popular among reders.
9. The **mountain** was covered with snow all the year round.
10. I'm going to be a **Newton** of Korea in the future.

〈참고〉 have a : 규칙 13 windows and : 규칙 28 all the : 규칙 16 year round : 규칙 17, 6 I'm going to : 규칙 27

발음규칙 10

[s] 뒤의 [k]는 모음 앞에서 된소리가 된다
[sk + 모음]

[s]음 다음에 [k]음이 오고 그 다음에 강모음이 오면 우리 글의 [ㅋ]으로 발음되지 않고 [ㄲ]으로 발음된다. 단어 또는 단어와 단어 사이에서 [k]앞에 강모음이 오면 된소리 [ㄲ]으로 발음된다.

WORD PRONUNCIATION PRACTICE

- ski   [스키-]   [스 끼-]
- skip over   [스킵 오우버]   [스 낍 오우-버ㄹ]
- skin   [스킨]   [스낀-]
- sky   [스카이]   [스까-이]
- schedule   [스케쥴]   [스께-쥬-ㄹ]
- school   [스쿨]   [스 꾸-ㄹ]
- square   [스퀘어]   [스꿰-어ㄹ]
- score   [스코어]   [스꼬-어ㄹ]
- ticket   [티켓]   [티-낏]
- pick it up   [픽 잇 압]   [피-끼 랍]
- take a loot at   [테이크 룩 앳]   [테-이꺼 (을)루 깻]

SENTENCE PRONUNCIATION PRACTICE

1. What do you think about going **skiing** with me?
2. When you don't know the answers on the test, **skip over** the questions.
3. Would you pass me the **skin** lotion?
4. The **sky** turned dark as the storm came near.
5. Could you tell me your **schedule**?
6. My school is located near the Youido **Square**.
7. The Korean soccer team won against the Japanese soccer team by a **score** of 3 to 1.
8. Why don't you take out the **ticket**?
9. Hey! Please **pick it up**.
10. **Take a look at** the map, please.

〈참고〉 what do you : 규칙 24   located : 규칙 1   near the : 규칙 16   take out : 규칙 10

발음규칙 11

[s] 뒤의 [p]는 모음 앞에서 된소리가 된다
[sp + 모음]

[s]음 다음에 [p]음이 오고 그 다음에 강모음이 오면 우리 글의 [ㅍ]으로 발음되지 않고 [ㅃ]으로 발음된다. 단어 또는 단어와 단어 사이에서 [p]앞에 강모음이 오면 된소리 [ㅃ]으로 발음된다.

WORD PRONUNCIATION PRACTICE

• spring	[스프링]	[스쁘―린]
• speak	[스픽]	[스삑]
• respect	[레스펙트]	[(우)리스빽―트]
• Spain	[스페인]	[스뻬―인]
• space	[스페이스]	[스뻬―이스]
• sport	[스폴트]	[스쁘―ㄹ트]
• spaghetti	[스파게티]	[스빠―게리]
• apple	[애플]	[애―쁘―ㄹ]
• happy	[해피]	[해―뻬]
• wrap it up	[랩 잇 앞]	[(우)래 뻬 랍]

SENTENCE PRONUNCIATION PRACTICE

1. The **spring** months are March, April, and May.
2. The best way to **speak** English well is to practice **speaking**.
3. My father was **respected** by everybody in my country.
4. Bullfighting is a form of public entertainment in **Spain**.
5. In the future, we will be able to travel to other planets in **space**.
6. Soccer is a **sport** everyone likes. The World Cup soccer games will be held in Korea and Japan in 2002.
7. My favorite food is **spaghetti**.
8. What would you like for dessert?   **Apples**, please.
9. I'm **happy** to see you again.
10. Could you **wrap it up** as soon as possible?

〈참고〉 April : 규칙 29 best way : 규칙 5 everybody : 규칙 2 Bullfighting : 규칙 1, 20 as soon : 규칙 17

발음규칙 12

[s] 뒤의 [t]는 모음 앞에서 된소리가 된다
[st + 모음]

[s]음 다음에 [t]음이 오고 그 다음에 강모음이 오면 우리 글의 [ㅌ]으로 발음되지 않고 [ㄸ]으로 발음된다. 단어 또는 단어와 단어 사이에서 [t]앞에 강모음이 오면 된소리 [ㄸ]으로 발음된다.

WORD PRONUNCIATION PRACTICE

• stop	[스톱]	[스땁]
• star	[스타]	[스따-ㄹ]
• student	[스튜던트]	[스뜌-(우)던(ㅌ)]
• mistake	[미스테이크]	[미스 떼-익]
• stay	[스테이]	[스떼-이]
• understand	[언더스탠드]	[언너ㄹ 스땐-]
• station	[스테이션]	[스떼-이션]
• doctor	[닥터]	[닥-떠ㄹ]
• taste of	[테이스트 오브]	[테-이스떠ㅂㅎ]
• date of	[데이트 오브]	[데-이떠ㅂㅎ]

SENTENCE PRONUNCIATION PRACTICE

1. In the future, just **stop** by any time you like.
2. It's great pleasure to meet a famous TV **star** like you.
3. I think Korean **students** study very hard.
4. Don't be afraid of making a **mistake** when speaking English.
5. Where will you be **staying**? I'm going to **stay** at my friend's.
6. I can't **understand** what you said. Please explain it in detail.
7. Excuse me, could you tell me the way to the subway **station**?
8. The **doctor** told me to take the medicine three times a day after meals.
9. The **taste of** the bean paste soup my mom cooked is very delicious.
10. Can you remember the **date of** our first meeting?

〈참고〉 In the : 규칙 16 like you : 규칙 15 think Korean : 규칙 17 study : 규칙 12 afraid of : 규칙 2 going to : 규칙 27 what you : 규칙 7

발음규칙 13 | 자음이 뒤의 모음에 어울려 소리난다
[자음 + 모음]

단어의 끝자음이 모음으로 시작되는 단어 앞에 오면 그 자음은
모음과 어울려서 발음된다. 이를 연음현상이라고 한다.

WORD PRONUNCIATION PRACTICE

• far away	[ㅍㅏㄹ 어웨이]	[ㅍ화 러웨이]
• for a long time	[ㅍ훠 어 롱 타임]	[ㅍ훠 러 롱 타임]
• half an hour	[해ㅍㅎ 언 아워]	[해 ㅍ훤 아ー우워ㄹ]
• have a cold	[해브 어 코울드]	[해 ㅂ허 콜드]
• think about	[싱크 어바우트]	[ㅎ 띵 꺼 바웃]
• thanks again	[쌩스 어게인]	[ㅎ 땡 써 겐]
• make it	[메이크 잇]	[메이 낏]
• Can I	[캔 아이]	[캐 나이]
• wrap it up	[랩 잇 업]	[(우)래뻬 랍]
• there is	[데얼 이즈]	[ㅎ데ー어ㄹ 리즈]

SENTENCE PRONUNCIATION PRACTICE

1. As she was **far away** from here, I couldn't recognize who she was.
2. I haven't seen you **for a long time**. I missed you.
3. How long does it take to get there?　　　　It takes about **half an hour**.
4. I'm like to take off tomorrow because I **have a** bad **cold**.
5. I can't **think about** it without crying.
6. You made me a model airplane for my homework. **Thanks again**.
7. I can't **make it** to the party. I have a previous appointment that day.
8. **Can** I keep it for a few weeks?
9. Here is Bob's Christmas gift. I have to **wrap it up** before the party.
10. **There is** a big tree in the center of the square.

〈참고〉 missed you : 규칙 7　does it : 규칙 24　takes about, for a : 규칙 13　before : 규칙 29　model : 규칙 2
keep it : 규칙 11　have to : 규칙 27　party : 규칙 3　center : 규칙 4

[s, z]가 [j]에 어울려 소리난다

[s, z + j]

단어와 단어 사이에서 자음 [s]나 [z] 뒤에 반모음 [j]가 오면
[s, + j ⇨ ʃ], [z + j ⇨ ʒ]로 발음된다. 자음과 반모음이 만나
다른 음으로 변하는 경향이 있다.

WORD PRONUNCIATION PRACTICE

• this year	[디스 이어]	[ㅎ디 쉬-어ㄹ]
• makes you	[메익스 유]	[메-익 슈]
• brush your	[브러쉬 유얼]	[브라-슈어ㄹ]
• wish you	[위쉬 유]	[위-슈]
• how's your	[하우즈 유얼]	[하-우 쥬어ㄹ]
• as you	[애즈 유]	[애 쥬]
• does your	[더즈 유어]	[더 쥬-어ㄹ]
• is your	[이즈 유얼]	[이 쥬-어ㄹ]
• was you	[워즈 유]	[워 쥬]
• knows you	[노우즈 유]	[노-우 쥬]

SENTENCE PRONUNCIATION PRACTICE

1. I have a plan to go abroad **this year**.
2. She always **makes you** happy.
3. **Brush your** hair everyday.
4. I **wish you** wouldn't be a trouble maker.
5. **How's your** family these days?   Everyone's fine.
6. **As you** know, I caught a cold this winter.
7. What **does your** father do?   He's an engineer.
8. **Is your** mother OK?   Yes, she's fine.
9. It **was you** that I saw in front of the theater at night.
10. He **knows you** are a professor at Seoul National University.

〈참고〉 have a : 규칙 13   wouldn't be : 규칙 6   trouble : 규칙 8   family : 규칙 29   caught a : 규칙 1   winter, front
of : 규칙 4   He's an : 규칙 13

발음규칙
15 | 자음이 [j]에 어울려 소리난다
[자음 + j]

단어와 단어 사이에서 자음 [v], [k], [p], [g], [f], [r] 등이 반모음 [j] 앞에 오면 붙여서 발음되는 경향이 있다.

WORD PRONUNCIATION PRACTICE

• have you	[해브 유]	[해 ㅂ휴]
• love you	[러브 유]	[(을)러 ㅂ휴]
• of you	[오 브 유]	[오 ㅂ휴]
• thank you	[쌩크 유]	[ㅎ땡 큐]
• pick you	[피크 유]	[피 뀨]
• take your	[테이크 유어]	[테-이 뀨어ㄹ]
• keep your	[키ㅍ 유얼]	[키 쀼어ㄹ]
• beg your	[벡 유얼]	[베 뀨어ㄹ]
• if you	[이흐 유]	[이 ㅍ휴]
• are you	[아유]	[아ㄹ 유]

SENTENCE PRONUNCIATION PRACTICE

1. **Have you** ever been to Canada?   Yes, I have.
2. I **love you** very much.
3. Some **of you** will receive my gifts.
4. I have to say **thank you** for your kindness.
5. I'll **pick you** up at seven p.m.
6. **Take your** time. Don't hurry.
7. Your mother will **keep your** money.
8. I **beg your** pardon. I can't hear you.
9. **If you** have no time, I'll stay at home all day.
10. What **are you** going to do tomorrow?

〈참고〉 been : 규칙 29   Some of : 규칙 26   have to, going to : 규칙 27   for you : 규칙 15   can't : 규칙 5   I'll stay : 규칙 25, 12   what are you : 규칙 23

발음규칙 16

[th]는 생략되면서 앞의 자음과 어울려 소리난다
[th(ð)음의 생략]

th[ð]음은 [s, z, l, n, r]음 뒤에서 발음이 안 되는 것처럼 들린다. [s + ð ⇨ s], [z + ð ⇨ z], [l + ð ⇨ l], [n + ð ⇨ n], [r + ð ⇨ r] 등으로 들린다.

WORD PRONUNCIATION PRACTICE

• what's the	[윗츠 더]	[윗-써]
• what's that	[윗츠 댓]	[윗-ㅆ앳]
• is this	[이즈 디스]	[이 지스]
• is there	[이즈 데어]	[이 제-어ㄹ]
• all the time	[올 더 타임]	[얼-러 타임]
• call that	[콜 댓]	[콜-랫]
• been there	[빈 데어]	[베ㄴ네어ㄹ]
• in the	[인 더]	[이 너]
• down there	[다운 데어]	[다-우 네어ㄹ]
• near the	[니어 더]	[니-어ㄹ러]
• hotter than	[핫터 댄]	[하ㄹ-러 랜]

SENTENCE PRONUNCIATION PRACTICE

1. **What's the** matter with you?
2. **What's that** mean?
3. **Is this** your car you bought last month?
4. **Is there** anybody looking for me?
5. In order to be healthy you must exercise **all the time**.
6. What do you **call that** in English?
7. Have you **been there** since I saw you last?   No, I have been **in the** United States.
8. Where are you going?   Oh, **down there**.
9. Where's your home?   My home's **near the** Chamsil Complex.
10. The climate of Taegu is **hotter than** that of Seoul.

〈참고〉 bought : 규칙 30   looking : 규칙 20   What do you : 규칙 24   United States : 규칙1, 12   Where are you going : 규칙 23, 20   of Taegu : 규칙 26

발음규칙 17 | 같은 자음이 겹치면 생략된다
[자음 + 자음] 1

두 개의 같은 자음이 겹치면 앞의 하나는 생략된다. 생략된 음의 길이만큼 끌어준다. [d + d ⇨ d], [f + f ⇨ f], [k + k ⇨ k], [l + l ⇨ l]

WORD PRONUNCIATION PRACTICE

• had dinner	[해드 디너]	[해(ㄷ) 디−너]
• cold day	[코울드 데이]	[콜−ㄹ(ㄷ) 데이]
• should do	[슈드 두]	[슈(ㄷ) 두]
• cold drink	[콜드 드링크]	[코−ㄹ(ㄷ) 쥬린ㅋ]
• wolf fighting	[울흐 파이팅]	[워−ㅍㅎ 화−이린]
• beef for dinner	[비흐 휘 디너]	[비−ㅍ휘 디−너ㄹ]
• speak Korean	[스픽 코리언]	[스삑 코리−언]
• dark colored	[다크 칼라드]	[다−ㄹㅋ 칼−라ㄹㄷ]
• All lions	[올 라이온즈]	[어−ㄹ− 라−이온즈]
• will leave	[윌 리브]	[위어−ㄹ 리−브]
• call later	[콜 레이터]	[코−ㄹ레−이러ㄹ]

SENTENCE PRONUNCIATION PRACTICE

1. I **had dinner** in a big restaurant on a **cold day**.
2. You **should do** your best even when you don't want to.
3. Excuse me, would you give me a **cold drink**?
4. Did you see the **wolf fighting** against the enormous moose?
5. Would you like to have **beef for dinner**?
6. Can you **speak Korean**?
7. That **dark colored** blouse looks very good on you.
8. **All lions** are fierce when they are hungry.
9. He **will leave** Seoul at the end of this month.
10. Okay, thank you. I'll **call later**.

〈참고〉 don't : 규칙 5 Did you, Would you : 규칙 7 good on : 규칙 2 end of : 규칙 13 I'll : 규칙 25

발음규칙 18 | 비슷한 자음이 겹치면 생략된다
[자음 + 자음] 2

두 개 자음 발음의 혀의 위치가 같거나 비슷할 때 앞 자음은 생략된다. 생략된 음의 길이만큼 끌어준다. [d + t ⇨ t], [t + d ⇨ d], [d + th ⇨ th], [t + th ⇨ th]

WORD PRONUNCIATION PRACTICE

• glad to	[글래드 투]	[글래-투]
• had to	[해드 투]	[해-러]
• round trip	[라운드 트리]	[라-운 추립]
• front desk	[후론트 데스크]	[프후론 데-스키]
• what do you	[윗 두 유]	[워 르유]
• must do	[머스트 두]	[머-스 두]
• found the	[화운드 더]	[프화-운 ㅎ너]
• behind the	[비인드 더]	[버하-인 ㅎ너]
• paint the	[페인트 더]	[페-인 ㅎ더]
• washed the	[워쉬트 더]	[워-쉬 ㅎ더]
• find the	[화인드 더]	[프화-인 ㅎ더]

SENTENCE PRONUNCIATION PRACTICE

1. **Glad to** meet you   **Glad to** meet you, too.
2. I **had to** keep a secret so that she would not be angry.
3. I want to get a **round trip** ticket for Toronto.
4. You'd better ask the lady about it at the **front desk**.
5. **What do you** want to do now?
6. You **must do** your homework right now.
7. I **found the** dog **behind the** hospital.
8. Could you **paint the** fence for me, please?
9. I **washed the** car yesterday because it was very dirty.
10. Go straight this way and you'll **find the** building.

〈참고〉 keep a : 규칙 11   Toronto : 규칙 4   about it : 규칙 1   want to : 규칙 29   dirty : 규칙 3   straight : 규칙 8
you'll : 규칙 25

발음규칙 19 | 자음이 3개 이상이면 중간 자음은 생략된다
[자음 + 자음 + 자음]

자음이 3개 또는 4개가 겹쳐질 때 중간 자음은 탈락되는 경향이 있다.

WORD PRONUNCIATION PRACTICE

• thanks	[생크스]	[ㅎ땡-스]
• stamps	[스템프스]	[스뗌-스]
• handkerchief	[핸드커치흐]	[행-커ㄹ치-ㅍ흐]
• West Point	[웨스트포인트]	[웨-스 포-인 트]
• sandwich	[쌘드위치]	[쌘-위치]
• recently	[리슨틀리]	[(우)릿-슨(을)리]
• postpone	[포스트폰]	[포-(우)스폰]
• chestnut	[체스너트]	[체-스넛]
• empty	[엠프티]	[엠-띠]
• attempt	[어템프트]	[어템-ㅌ]
• postcard	[포스트 카드]	[포-스 카ㅡㄹㄷ]

SENTENCE PRONUNCIATION PRACTICE

1. Have a seat here.   **Thanks** a lot.
2. My brother in **West Germany** collected a lot of foreign **stamps**.
3. I bought a white **handkerchief** for my boy friend at **West Point**.
4. I'd like to have a **sandwich** with a coke.
5. How have you been **recently**?   Pretty good.
6. Do you mind if I **postpone** that appointment until next week?
7. We won the **hand ball** game 25 to 20 against Hong Kong.
8. In autumn there are a lot of **chestnuts** in the mountains.
9. Could you give me an **empty** envelope?
10. He made no **attempt** to escape from the prison.

〈참고〉 Have a : 규칙 13 Do you : 규칙 24 mind : 규칙 4 appointment, next week : 규칙 5 autumn : 규칙 1 in the : 규칙 16 mountains : 규칙 9

발음규칙 20 | 빠른 대화에서[-ing]의 "g"는 생략된다
[-ing의 g 생략]

빠른 대화에서 [ing]의 [g]음이 탈락되고, [-in]으로 발음된다.
이때 [-ing] 다음에 모음으로 시작되는 단어가 오면 연음된다.

WORD PRONUNCIATION PRACTICE

• staying	[스테잉]	[스떼-인]
• getting	[게팅]	[게-린]
• something	[썸싱]	[썸 ㅅ띤]
• nothing	[낙싱]	[낙 ㅅ띤]
• coming	[컴잉]	[카-민]
• going	[고-잉]	[고-인]
• doing	[두-잉]	[두-인]
• looking	[룩킹]	[(을)룩-낀]
• going on	[고잉 온]	[고-이 넌]
• going to	[고잉 투]	[고 너]

SENTENCE PRONUNCIATION PRACTICE

1. Where will you be **staying**?　　　　　　　　At my friend's.
2. How are you **getting** along in this hot season?　I'm fine.
3. I have **something** to tell you.
4. I have **nothing** to do now.　　　　　　　　I'm very bored.
5. Is he **coming** soon?　　　　　　　　　　Yes, sir.
6. How's it **going**?　　　　　　　　　　　Pretty good.
7. How are you **doing**?　　　　　　　　　　I'm **doing** well.
8. What are you **looking** for?　　　　　　　I'm **looking** for a motel to stay in.
9. What's **going on**?　　　　　　　　　　Nothing much.
10. What are you **going to** do next weekend?　I'm **going to** take a trip to Pusan.

〈참고〉 will you : 규칙 15　Yes, sir : 규칙 17　How's it : 규칙 23　for a : 규칙 13　next weekend : 규칙 5, 6　take a
　　　 trip : 규칙 10, 8

발음규칙 21 | [h]는 약모음 앞에서 자주 생략된다
["h"음의 생략]

빠른 대화 속에서 [h]음은 약모음 앞에서 생략되는 경향이 있다. [h]음은 탈락되면서 앞 단어와 연음된다.

WORD PRONUNCIATION PRACTICE

• tell him	[텔 힘]	[텔 림]
• come here	[컴 히어]	[카 미-어ㄹ]
• her name	[헐 네임]	[어ㄹ 네-임]
• what's he	[웟즈 히]	[웟 씨]
• did he	[디드 히]	[디 리]
• to him	[투 힘]	[터 임]
• with him	[위드 힘]	[위ㄷ 림]
• give him	[기브 힘]	[기-ㅂㅎ임]
• leave her	[리브 허]	[(을)리-ㅂ허ㄹ]
• stop him	[스톱 힘]	[스따 쁨]

SENTENCE PRONUNCIATION PRACTICE

1. Please **tell him** I'm here.
2. **Come here** quickly.
3. I don't know **her name**.
4. **What's he** going to do?
5. When **did he** call me?
6. What do you want to do?　　　　　I want to talk **to him**.
7. What would you like to have for lunch **with him**?
8. Would you give him something to drink?
9. Please **leave her** alone.
10. We've got to **stop him** right now.

〈참고〉 I'm here : 규칙 21 going to : 규칙 27 What do you : 규칙 24 have for : 규칙 18 something to drink : 규칙 20, 8 got to : 규칙 17, 1

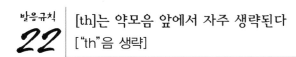

발음규칙 22 | [th]는 약모음 앞에서 자주 생략된다 ["th"음 생략]

th[ð]음은 바른 속도로 말할 때 약모음 앞에서 생략되는 경향이 있다. [ð]음은 탈락되면서 앞 단어와 연음된다.

WORD PRONUNCIATION PRACTICE

• pick them up	[픽 뎀 압]	[픽 껨 압]
• let them	[렛 뎀]	[(을)레-럼, (을)룩-럼]
• told them	[토울드 뎀]	[토-ㄹ럼]
• some of them	[썸 오브 뎀]	[써-머 범]
• all of them	[올 오브 뎀]	[어-ㄹ러범]
• sell them	[쎌 뎀]	[쎄-ㄹ럼]
• both of them	[보우스 오브 뎀]	[보-써범]
• saw them	[쏘우 뎀]	[써-엄]
• look at them	[룩 애ㄷ 뎀]	[(을)룩 애-럼]
• make them	[메이크 뎀]	[메-이껨]

SENTENCE PRONUNCIATION PRACTICE

1. Would you **pick them up** at seven in the evening?
2. **Let them** read the English book over and over again.
3. I **told them** to find out if he's still staying there.
4. **Some of them** have been working on the same job for ten years.
5. **All of them** are trying to get a new job.
6. Many department stores **sell them** on sale in October.
7. **Both of them** are wrong on the questions.
8. I **saw them** in front of the National Museum a couple of weeks ago.
9. Don't **look at them** now. They'll recognize you at once.
10. You've got to **make them** help one another.

〈참고〉 over and : 규칙 13 find out, front of : 규칙 4 staying there : 규칙 20, 16 couple of : 규칙 26 You've : 규칙 25 got to : 규칙 17, 1

발음규칙 23

be동사와 같이 쓰일 때의 여러 가지 발음
[be 동사의 축약 현상]

[be + 주어]나 [의문사 + be + 주어]는 축약시켜서 한 덩어리로 발음되는 경향이 있다.

WORD PRONUNCIATION PRACTICE

• am I	[엠 아이]]	[어 마-이]]
• What am I	[윗 엠 아이]]	[워러 마-이]]
• are you	[아 유]	[아르유-]
• What are you	[윗 아 유]	[워 러유-]
• Where are you	[웨얼 아 유]	[웨-어 러유-]
• is he	[이즈 히]	[이 지-]
• was she	[워즈 쉬]	[워 쉬-]
• is this	[이즈 디스]	[이 지-스]
• is it	[이즈 이트]	[이 짓]
• How's it	[하우즈 이트]	[하-우 짓]

SENTENCE PRONUNCIATION PRACTICE

1. **Am I** really seventeen?
2. **What am I** going to be in the future?
3. **Are you** OK?
4. **What are you** talking about?
5. **Where are you** going to stay?
6. **Is he** coming soon?
7. Why **was she** absent from the meeting?
8. **Is this** your first visit to Korea?
9. **Is it** possible to get there within an hour?
10. **How's it** going?

〈참고〉 going to : 규칙 27 in the : 규칙 16 talking about : 규칙 20, 13 absent : 규칙 5 meeting : 규칙 20 first visit : 규칙 5 within an : 규칙 13

발음규칙 24 | do, does, did 동사와 같이 쓰일 때의 여러 가지 발음 [do, does, did 축약 현상]

[do, does, did + 주어]와 [의문사 + do, does, did + 주어]는 한 덩어리로 발음되는 경향이 있다.

WORD PRONUNCIATION PRACTICE

• What do you	[윗 두 유]	[워 르유]
• Where do you	[웨어 두 유]	[웨-어 르유]
• How do you	[하우 두 유]	[하-우 르유]
• does he	[더즈 히]	[더 지]
• What does she	[윗 더즈 쉬]	[윗 더-쉬]
• does it	[더즈 잇]	[더 짓]
• did he	[디드 히]	[디 리-]
• What did you	[윗 디드 유]	[윗 디쥬-]
• When did you	[웬 디드 유]	[웬 디쥬-]
• did it	[디드 잇]	[디 릿]

SENTENCE PRONUNCIATION PRACTICE

1. **What do you** mean?　　　　　　Nothing.
2. **Where do you** want to go?
3. **How do you** do?　　　　　　　Nice meeting you.
4. **Does he** live near here?　　　　I don't know where he lives.
5. **What does she** want to do?
6. **Does it** take a long time to get there?
7. **Did he** have a good time last weekend?
8. **What did you** like to do?
9. **When did you** change your mind?
10. **Did it** snow last night?

〈참고〉 want to : 규칙 27　meeting : 규칙 20　near here : 규칙 21　take a, have a : 규칙 10　last night : 규칙 5

발음규칙 25 | 주어와 동사의 준말의 여러 가지 발음
[준말의 축약 현상]

말을 할 때 [주어 + 동사]를 줄여서 발음하는 경향이 있다.

WORD PRONUNCIATION PRACTICE

• I'll	[아일]	[아이-어-ㄹ]
• I'd	[아이드]	[아이-ㄷ]
• I've	[아이브]	[아이-ㅂㅎ]
• You'll	[유일]	[유-어-ㄹ]
• You'd	[유드]	[유-ㄷ]
• You've	[유브]	[유-ㅂㅎ]
• He'll	[힐]	[히-어-ㄹ]
• She'll	[쉴]	[쉬-어-ㄹ]
• It'll	[잇를]	[이-러-ㄹ]
• That'll	[댓를]	[대-러-ㄹ]

SENTENCE PRONUNCIATION PRACTICE

1. **I'll** be there in ten m̲inutes.
2. **I'd** like to join you for dinner this Saturday.
3. **I've** g̲o̲t̲ ̲t̲o̲ go home right now.
4. **You'll** do well i̲f̲ ̲y̲ou try.
5. **You'd** better go see a doctor right now.
6. **You've** known the facts, haven̲'t you?
7. **He'll** cal̲l̲ ̲you back soon.
8. **She'll** get wel̲l̲ ̲i̲n̲ ̲a̲ few days.
9. **It'll** clear̲ ̲u̲p̲ soon.
10. **That'll** be very nice.

〈참고〉 m̲inutes : 규칙 29   g̲o̲t̲ ̲t̲o̲ : 규칙 1, 17   i̲f̲ ̲y̲ou, cal̲l̲ ̲y̲ou : 규칙 15   haven̲'t you : 규칙 7   wel̲l̲ : 규칙 31   i̲n̲ ̲a̲,
clear̲ ̲u̲p̲ : 규칙 13

발음규칙 26 | [of]의 "f"는 약음되어 소리가 나지 않는다
[of 약음의 축약 현상]

of의 [v]음은 자음 앞에서 거의 탈락되고 모음 앞에서 모음에
연음되어 이동된다.

WORD PRONUNCIATION PRACTICE

• a cup of coffee	[어 컵 어브 커휘]	[어 카퍼 커–ㅍ휘]
• a glass of milk	[어 글래스 오브 밀크]	[어 글래–써 미–억]
• another pair of shoes	[어나더 패얼 오브 슈즈]	[어나–ㅎ덜 페–어러 슈–즈]
• a lot of traffic	[어 랏 오브 트래휙]	[어 (을)라–러 츄래–ㅍ휙]
• get out of here	[케트 아우트오브 히어]	[게라–러 히–어리]
• a couple of weeks	[어 카풀 오브 웍스]	[어 카–풀러 웍–스]
• all of a sudden	[올 오브 어 써든]	[어–러버 써–ㅅ은]
• first of all	[휠스트 오브 올]	[ㅍ휘–ㄹ스트 어버 어–ㄹ]
• out of a job	[아우트 오브 어 쟈ㅂ]	[아우 러버 쟙]
• all of you	[올 오브 유]	[어–ㄹ 러 ㅂ휴]

SENTENCE PRONUNCIATION PRACTICE

1. Would you care for **a cup of coffee**?   Yes, please.
2. Would you like **a glass of milk**?   Thank you very much.
3. May I show you **another pair of shoes**?   A larger one, please.
4. I was late for the party because of **a lot of traffic**.
5. I hate you. **Get out of here** right now.
6. My sister will get married in **a couple of weeks**.
7. It's really dark out there. **All of a sudden** it's really pouring.
8. We've very hungry. **First of all** we'd better look for a restaurant.
9. He was **out of a job**. He's looking for a new job now.
10. **All of you** will be in charge of the project.

〈참고〉 Thank you : 규칙 15 for the : 규칙 16, 13 hate you : 규칙 7 will : 규칙 31 out there : 규칙 18 looking : 규
칙 20 for a : 규칙 13

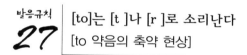

[to]는 [t]나 [r]로 소리난다
[to 약음의 축약 현상]

to[tu]는 약음화 되어 [t]나 [r]로 발음된다. [going to + V], [have to], [has to], [want to], [wants to], [used to] 등이 있다.

WORD PRONUNCIATION PRACTICE

- going to be   [고잉 투 비]   [거–너 비]
- going to stay   [고잉 투 스테이]   [거–너 스떼–이]
- going to make   [고잉 투 메이크]   [거–너 메–익]
- trying to get   [트라잉 투 겟]   [츄라–이너 겟]
- have to go   [해브 투 고]   [해–ㅍ후터 고]
- has to leave   [해즈 투 리브]   [해–즈터 리–ㅂ흐]
- want to do   [원투 투 두]   [워–너 두]
- want to postpone   [원투 포스트 폰]   [워–너 포(우)–스폰]
- wants to take   [원츠 투 테이크]   [원–츠 터 테–익]
- used to be   [유스트 투 비]   [유–스터 비]

SENTENCE PRONUNCIATION PRACTICE

1. What are you **going to be** in the future?
2. How long are you **going to stay** in Seoul?
3. Where are you **going to make a** trip this year?
4. I'm **trying to get** a new job suitable for me.
5. Do I **have to go** to college in the future?
6. Something urgent has come up, and he **has to leave** for New York.
7. What do you **want to do** now?
8. I **want to postpone** that appointment until next week. Are you OK?
9. He **wants to take** me out for dinner this evening.
10. There **used to be** a statue in the center of the square.

〈참고〉 What are you, where are you : 규칙 23   make a : 규칙 10   go to : 규칙 1   What do you : 규칙 24   in the center : 규칙 4, 16

발음규칙 28

[and]가 [n]으로 앞 단어에 끌려서 소리나고, [or]는 앞 단어에 끌려서 소리난다

[and와 or의 축약 현상]

and와 or는 빠른 속도로 말할 때 and의 d가 탈락되어 [ər, n] 으로, or는 [ər]로 약화되어 둘 다 발음은 앞 단어에 끌려간다.

WORD PRONUNCIATION PRACTICE

• you and I	[유 앤드 아이]	[유 은 아-이]
• bread and butter	[브레드 앤드 버터]	[브래-든 버-러ㄹ]
• black and white	[블랙 앤드 화이트]	[블랙-은 와-잇]
• come and see	[콤 앤드 씨]	[캄은 씨]
• up and down	[엎 앤드 다운]	[압쁜 다-운]
• cats and dogs	[캣츠 앤드 독즈]	[캣츤 더ㄱ-스]
• Bill and Tom	[빌 앤드 톰]	[빌-른 탐]
• coffee or ten	[커휘 오얼 티]	[커-ㅍ휘 어ㄹ 티]
• now or later	[나우 오얼 레이터]	[나-우 어ㄹ (을)레-이러]
• to go or to eat	[투 고 오얼 투 이트]	[투 고 어ㄹ 투 잇]

SENTENCE PRONUNCIATION PRACTICE

1. **You and I** have got to paint the fence by this Saturday.
2. May I bring you some **bread and butter** with a glass of milk?
3. The colors used in chess are **black and white**.
4. I hope you will **come and see** me some day.
5. The elevator goes **up and down** in the department store.
6. It's raining **cats and dogs**.
7. I'm going to invite **Bill and Tom** to my birthday party.
8. Would you like **coffee or tea**?
9. Do you want to do your homework **now or later**?
10. Would you like this pizza **to go or to eat** here?

〈참고〉 got to : 규칙 17, 1   paint : 규칙 5   glass of milk : 규칙 26   in the : 규칙 16   I'm going to : 규칙 27   party : 규칙 3   want to do : 규칙 27   Would you : 규칙 7

발음규칙 29

[i]는 강세가 없으면 [ə]로, [i]는 강세가 있으면 [e]로 소리난다
[i의 약음의 축약 훈련]

i 발음은 강음절 뒤나 앞에서 [ə]로 약화되거나 탈락되는 경향
이 있다. i 발음에 강세가 오면 [e]로 발음되고, 강세가 오지
않으면 [ə]로 발음된다.

WORD PRONUNCIATION PRACTICE

• April	[에이프릴]	[에-이 쁘러-ㄹ]
• holiday	[홀리데이]	[할-러데이]
• impossible	[임파씨블]	[임파-써브-ㄹ]
• terrible	[테리블]	[테-러브-ㄹ]
• pencil	[펜실]	[펜-써-ㄹ]
• before	[비ㅍ훠ㄹ]	[버ㅍ훠-ㄹ]
• sit down	[쎄ㅅ 다운]	[쎄ㅅ 다운]
• swim	[스윔]	[스웸]
• been	[빈]	[벤]
• minute	[미니트]	[메-넷]

SENTENCE PRONUNCIATION PRACTICE

1. Which do you like better, **April** or August?

2. Where are you going for the **holiday**?

3. It's **impossible** to postpone our plan to go on a trip.

4. How about the traffic in Seoul?　　Wow! The traffic is **terrible**!

5. Where's my **pencil**?　　It's under the table. Please pick it up.

6. I've seen you **before**, haven't I?

7. Why don't you **sit down**?　　I have something to tell you.

8. I go **swimming** for my health every morning.

9. Where have you **been** recently?　　I've been in the country.

10. Wait a **minute**. I'll be there soon.

〈참고〉 postpone : 규칙 19　pick it up : 규칙 1　something : 규칙 20　have you : 규칙 13　recently : 규칙 9　I've
been : 규칙 25, 29　Wait a : 규칙 1　I'll be : 규칙 25

발음규칙 30

[ɔ]가 [ɑ]로 소리난다
[ɔ] ⇨ [ɑ] 발음 훈련

미국식 발음에서 [ɔ]음에 강세가 올 때 [ɑ]음으로 발음되는 경향이 있다. [ɔ] ⇨ [ɑ]

WORD PRONUNCIATION PRACTICE

• philosophy	[프휘라–쏘프휘]	• modern	[마–런]
• daughter	[다–러ㄹ]	• doll	[다–ㄹ]
• contest	[칸–테스트]	• concert	[칸–써ㄹ트]
• college	[카–을리쥐]	• hospital	[하–스뻐러–ㄹ]
• jog	[자–그]	• comedy	[카–머리]
• promise	[프(우)라–미스]	• opera	[아–퍼(우)러]
• Toronto	[투(우)라–노]	• opportunity	[아–퍼ㄹ튜–니디]
• helicopter	[헬–리캅프터ㄹ]	• occupation	[아–큐페–이션]
• operate	[아–퍼(우)레잇]	• bottom	[바–럼]
• bottle	[바–르–ㄹ]	• possible	[파–써브–ㄹ]
• rocket	[(우)라–킷]		

SENTENCE PRONUNCIATION PRACTICE

1. We need a **philosophy** to be successful in this **modern** society.
2. My **daughter's** hobby is collecting **dolls**.
3. There used to be a piano **contest** at the **concert** hall.
4. Is there a **college** next to the **hospital**?
5. Watching a fat man **jog** is like watching a **comedy**.
6. My father **promised** to take me to the **opera** house in **Toronto**.
7. I had an **opportunity** to fly a **helicopter**.
8. His new **occupation** is to **operate** a machine.
9. I found a piece of paper at the **bottom** of the **bottle**.
10. In the future, it may be **possible** to go from Seoul to New York by **rocket** ship in an hour.

〈참고〉 need a, had an : 규칙 2 used to : 규칙 27 Is there : 규칙 16 found a : 규칙 4 piece of : 규칙 26 in an hour : 규칙 13

발음규칙
31

[l] 발음에 [ə]를 첨가하여 발음한다
[l] 발음 [ə] 첨가 발음훈련

[l]음이 모음 뒤에 오면서 단어 끝이나 자음 앞에 오면 [ə]를 넣어서 발음하고 l은 발음되지 않는다. 하지만 모음 앞에 오면 [l]음을 낸다. (예 : light ⇨ (을)라잇)

WORD PRONUNCIATION PRACTICE

• will	[윌]	[위-어-ㄹ]
• style	[스타일]	[스따-이어-ㄹ]
• detail	[디테일]	[디테-이어-ㄹ]
• oil	[오일]	[오-이어-ㄹ]
• oatmeal	[오트밀]	[오-트미어-ㄹ]
• film	[필림]	[프휘-엄]
• milk	[밀크]	[미-어ㅋ]
• help	[헬프]	[헤-어ㅍ]
• golf	[골프]	[고-ㅍㅎ]
• full-time	[프흘타임]	[프후-ㄹ 타임]

SENTENCE PRONUNCIATION PRACTICE

1. **Will** you have time to <u>go to</u> see a movie this evening?   <u>I'm</u> afraid not.
2. John wrote a poem in a different **style**.
3. I don't know <u>what you</u> mean. Please explain it to me in **detail**.
4. My father works for an **oil** company.
5. The **oatmeal** is <u>on the</u> table <u>behind you</u>. Help yourself, please.
6. I <u>want to</u> get some **film**.   That be all?   <u>That's it</u>.
7. May I have another glass of **milk**?
8. I appreciate your **help**. I can't thank you enough.
9. He stopped playing **golf** because of the recession this year.
10. Do you want a **full-time** job or a part-time job?

〈참고〉 <u>go to</u> : 규칙 1 <u>I'm</u> : 규칙 23 wh<u>at you</u> : 규칙 7 <u>on the</u> : 규칙 16 beh<u>ind you</u> : 규칙 7 <u>want to</u> : 규칙 27
<u>That's it</u> : 규칙 23

발음규칙 32 | 단어에 따라 강약이 주어진다
[문장의 강약 연습]

내용어인 명사, 동사, 형용사, 부사, 지시대명사, 의문사 등은 강하게 발음하고, 기능어인 관사, 전치사, 인칭대명사, 관계대명사, 접속사, be동사, 조동사 등은 약하게 발음한다. 전치사 + 관사 + 명사 ⇨ [중 + 약 + 강] / 동사 + 대명사 ⇨ [강 + 약] 명사 + to 부정사 ⇨ [강 + 약] / 타동사 + 목적어 ⇨ [약 + 강]

WORD PRONUNCIATION PRACTICE

• at the store	[앳 더 스토아]	[앳 더 스또-어ㄹ]
• by the front desk	[바이 더 프론트 데스크]	[바이 더 ㅍㅎ론 데스ㅋ]
• in the park	[인더 파크]	[이너 파-ㄹㅋ]
• invite him	[인바이트 힘]	[인ㅂ하-이 림]
• send it	[쎈드 이트]	[쎄-닛]
• something to tell	[썸씽 투 텔]	[썸ㅎ띤 투 테어-ㄹ]
• water to drink	[워터 투 드링크]	[워-러ㄹ 투 쥬린ㅋ]
• what to do	[워ㅌ 투 두]	[윗 투두]
• need your help	[니드 유얼 헬프]	[니-쥐ㄹ 헤-업]
• buy a computer	[바이 어 컴퓨터]	[바-이어 컴퓨-러ㄹ]

SENTENCE PRONUNCIATION PRACTICE

(강세가 있는 내용어는 모두 굵은 글자로 처리하였습니다.)

1. I **bought** a **lot** of **things** at the **store** for our **picnic**.
2. Do you **know who** the **man** is by the **front** desk?
3. There was a **wedding** in the **park** a **week ago**.
4. Would you **like** to **invite** him to your **birthday** party?
5. I'd like to **send** it to you during my **summer** vacation.
6. I have **something** to tell you. Come **on in**, please.
7. We have no **water** to drink. We must be **patient**.
8. I don't **know what** to do next.
9. I **need** your **help**. Please **call** me **back** as soon as **possible**.
10. I **want** to buy a **computer** today, but I don't **have** enough **money**.

〈참고〉 lot of : 규칙 1, 26 send it : 규칙 4, on in : 규칙 13 water to drink : 규칙 1, 8 must be : 규칙 5 patient : 규칙 4 your help : 규칙 31 as soon as : 규칙 17

발음규칙 33 [띄어읽기 연습]

1. 쉼표(컴머)가 있으면 반드시 띄어읽는다.
2. 주부와 술부 사이에 띄어읽는다.
3. 절과 절 사이에 띄어읽는다.
4. 부사구 앞에서 띄어읽는다.
※ 주부에 주어가 하나 있으면 띄어읽지 않는다.
　주부가 너무 길면 그 안에서 띄어읽는다.

SENTENCE PRONUNCIATION PRACTICE

1. I go to school / today.
2. He was at home / at seven in the evening.
3. She went to America / to study music / last year.
4. There was a man / waiting for you.
5. I was watching TV / when my mom came into my room.
6. You look happy / this morning.
7. All the leaves in the mountain / turn red and yellow / in autumn.
8. She was very surprised / to hear the news.
9. It is impossible / to master English / in a year.
10. I need your help / to operate this machine.
11. Leave me alone, please. / I want to think about it / for a while.
12. I can't understand / what you said.
13. I don't know the reason / why she left me.
14. Do you know the lady / who is singing / on the stage?
15. He sent me many books / a couple of weeks ago.
16. We call him / the Newton of Korea.
17. She made me happy / the last ten years.
18. He wants me to paint the fence / by this time tomorrow.
19. I saw him write a letter / in English.
20. I saw a fat woman running / along the street.

4. Core Vocabulary (핵심 어휘)

핵심어휘를 공부해야 듣기가 된다.

[이런 단어 알아야 듣기가 된다

― Listening에 익혀야 될 어휘와 표현]

① DIRECTIONS (길 묻기)

- **traffic light** 신호등
- **crosswalk / ped crossing** 횡단보도
- **intersection** 사거리
- **corner** 모퉁이
- **block** 구역
- **sidewalk** 보도
- **pedestrian** 보행자
- **detour / bypass** 우회도로
- **Avenue** 큰 거리(남북)
- **Street** 거리(동서)

- **express way / free way** 고속도로
- **highway** (차량이 많이 다니는)넓은 도로
- **Go ahead.** 앞으로 가세요.
- **Go straight.** 똑바로 가세요.
- **Take a bus.** 버스를 타세요.
- **get on** 타다
- **get off** 내리다
- **Turn right.** 오른쪽으로 도세요.
- **Make a right.** 오른쪽으로 가세요.
- **Make a detour.** 우회하세요.

- You can't miss it. 틀림없이 찾을 수 있을 것입니다.
- Could you tell me the way ~? (~에 가는 길을 말씀해 주시겠습니까?)
- How can I get to ~? (~에 어떻게 갈 수 있습니까?)
- How long does it take to ~? (~에 가는 데 얼마나 걸립니까?)
- It takes about five minutes to get ~. (~에 가는 데 약 5분 걸립니다.)

② TRAFFIC (교통)

- **vehicle** 차량
- **lane** 차선
- **overpass** 고가도로
- **underpass** 지하도
- **bus stop** 버스 정류장
- **subway No. 2 line** 지하철 2호선
- **taxi stand** 택시 승차장

- **heavy traffic** 교통 혼잡
- **traffic accident** 교통사고
- **shortcut** 지름길
- **parking lot** 주차장
- **illegal parking** 불법주차
- **pull over** 차를 길가로 붙이다
- **pull up** 차를 멈추다

- **rest area** 휴게소
- **fare** 운임
- **toll** 통행료
- **traffic jam** 교통체증

- **take off** 이륙하다
- **land** 착륙하다
- **board** 탑승하다, 승선하다
- **aboard** 타고 있는

③ TELEPHONE (전화)

- **phone booth(box)** 전화박스
- **pay(public) phone** 공중전화
- **touch-tone phone** 전자식 전화기
- **cordless phone** 무선 전화기
- **cellular phone / cell phone** 휴대폰
- **phone book** 전화번호 책
- **telephone directory** 전화번호 책
- **white pages** 개인별 전화번호부
- **yellow pages** 업종별 전화번호부
- **slot** 동전 주입구
- **operator** 교환수
- **local call** 시내전화 (통화 시작부터 요금이 부과된다)

- **long-distance call** 시외전화
- **overseas (international) call** 국제전화
- **country code** 국가번호
- **area code** 지역번호
- **hot line** 긴급 직통전화
- **extension number** 교환 전화번호
- **telephone charge** 전화요금
- **telephone bill** 전화요금 고지서
- **collect call** 수신자 부담 전화
- **person-to person call** 지명통화
- **station-to-station call** 보통통화

- **deposit** 동전을 전화기 또는 자판기에 넣다
- **look it up** 전화 번호부에서 이름과 번호를 찾다
- **make a call / call / phone** 전화 걸다
- **hang up / disconnect** 전화를 끊다
- **hold on / hold the line** 전화를 들고 기다리다
- **be on another phone / talk on another line** 다른 전화를 받다
- **The line is busy. / be still on the line** 통화중이다
- **leave a message** 메시지를 남기다
- **take a message** 메시지를 받다
- **You have the wrong number.** 전화 잘못 하셨습니다
- **This is Thomas speaking. = Thomas speaking. = This is he.** 토마스입니다
- **Who's calling please? = Who's this please?** 누구시지요?
- **May I speak to ~? / I'd like to speak to ~.** ~를 바꿔주세요

④ AT A RESTAURANT (식당에서)

- **dish / plate** 접시

- **scrambled** 풀어서 익힌

- **dish / food** 요리
- **bowl** 사발, 공기
- **cup and saucer** 컵과 받침 접시
- **dressing** 소스(여러 가지 재료)
- **sauce** 소스(한가지 재료)
- **sirloin steal** 등심 스테이크
- **rare** 덜 구워진
- **medium** 중간 정도로 구운
- **well-done** 바싹 구운
- **roast** 오븐에 구운
- **grilled** 석쇠에 구운
- **smoked** 훈제의
- **steamed** 찐

- **hard boiled** 완전히 삶은
- **soft boiled** 반숙
- **sunny-side up** 한 쪽만 후라이한 것
- **over easy** 양 쪽 다 후라이한 것
- **beverage = drink** 음료(물 이외의)
- **soft drink** 비 알콜성 음료
- **strong drink** 알콜성 음료
- **liquor** 독한 술(위스키와 같은)
- **on the rocks** 얼음을 넣은 (술에)
- **straight up** 얼음을 넣지 않은
- **vegetarian** 채식주의자
- **decaf** 카페인이 없는 커피
- **diet soda** 무설탕 음료수

- I'd like to run a tab. / It's on me. / It's my treat. 제가 계산할게요.
- I'm on a diet. 다이어트 중인데요.
- take your time. 천천히 드세요.
- Are you ready to order? / Can I take your order? 주문하시겠습니까?
- Would you like to have ~? ~를 드시겠습니까?
- Would you care for (like) ~? ~ 드시겠습니까?
- What would you like for ~? ~으로 뭘 드시겠습니까?
- How would you like ~? ~을 어떻게 드시겠습니까?
- Help yourself. / Enjoy your meal. 맛있게 드세요

⑤ VEGETABLES (야채)

- **spinach** 시금치
- **carrot** 당근
- **pumpkin** 호박
- **mushroom** 버섯
- **onion** 양파
- **potato** 감자
- **sweet potato** 고구마

- **cabbage** 양배추
- **red pepper** 고추
- **eggplant** 가지
- **lettuce** 상추
- **cucumber** 오이
- **turnip** 무
- **radish** 빨간 무

⑥ COOK (요리)

- **swallow** 삼키다

- **gulp** 꿀꺽 삼키다

- **sip** 홀짝 홀짝 마시다
- **chew** 씹다
- **quench** 갈증을 풀다
- **roast** 굽다(오븐에)
- **mash** 으깨다(찐 감자를)
- **whip** 휘저어 거품을 내다
- **grate** 강판으로 갈다
- **peel** 껍질을 벗기다

- **drink** 마시다
- **devour** 게걸스럽게 먹다
- **steam** 찌다(음식을)
- **stir** 휘젓다(액체를)
- **crush** 가루로 만들다
- **slice** 얇게 베어내다
- **chop** 잘게 썰다
- **pour** 붓다

⑦ AT A BANK (은행에서)

- **banker** 은행인
- **teller / bank clerk** 은행 금전 출납인
- **bankbook / passbook** 예금통장
- **savings account** 저축예금, 보통예금
- **checking account** 당좌예금
- **account number** 은행계좌 번호
- **deposit** 예금(하다)
- **deposit slip** 입금표
- **withdraw** 인출하다
- **cash** 현찰
- **check** 수표, 계산서
- **bill** 지폐, 청구서
- **change** 잔돈
- **money-transfer** 송금

- **savings** 저축
- **balance** 잔고
- **interests** 이자
- **interest rate** 이자율
- **overdue** 연체된
- **exchange office** 환전소
- **pawn** 담보물
- **pension** 연금
- **withdrawal** 인출
- **withdrawal slip** 인출금표
- **fill out** 작성하다
- **fake money** 위조지폐
- **service-charge** 수수료

- I'd like to open an account. 예금계좌를 개설하고 싶습니다.
- He drew out all his savings. 그는 자기 예금을 모두 찾았습니다.

⑧ AT A POST OFFICE (우체국에서)

- **mail** 우편, 우편으로 부치다
- **airmail** 항공우편
- **surface mail** 선박요금
- **stamp** 우표
- **postcard** 그림엽서

- **postage** 우편요금
- **surcharge** 추가요금
- **domestic mail** 국내 우편
- **express mail** 속달 우편
- **registered mail** 등기우편

- parcel 소포
- package 소포
- zip code 우편번호
- sender 발신인
- addressee 수신인
- ten 150 won stamps 150원 우표 10장
- direct mail 광고 우편물
- special delivery 속달
- by express 속달로
- money order 우편환
- fragile 깨지기 쉬운
- postscript 추신

⑨ SHAPE / PICTURE (도형)

- circle 원
- square 사각형
- triangle 삼각형
- rectangle 직사각형
- cube 정육면체
- dot 점
- line 선
- side 변
- flat 평평한
- round 둥근
- top 꼭대기
- bottom 밑바닥, 아래
- diameter 지름
- radius 반지름
- draw 그리다
- describe 설명하다

- A triangle is a shape with three sides. 삼각형에는 세 변이 있습니다.
- A square has four sides. 정사각형에는 네 변이 있습니다.
- A rectangle has two short sides and two long sides. 직사각형은 두 개의 짧은 변과 두 개의 긴 변으로 이루어져 있습니다.
- The line from one side of a circle to the other side is the diameter. 원의 한 변에서 다른 변에 이르는 선이 지름입니다.
- We call the line from the outside of a circle to the center of the circle the radius. 원의 바깥쪽에서 중심에 이르는 선을 반지름이라고 합니다.

⑩ TOUR (여행)

- sightseeing 관광
- travel agency 여행사
- travel agent 여행사 직원
- brochure 안내서
- departure 출발
- arrival 도착
- one-way ticket 편도표
- round-trip ticket 왕복표
- traveler's check 여행자 수표
- destination 행선지, 목적지
- resort 휴양지
- interesting place 관광명소
- souvenir store 기념품 가게
- outlook 전망
- confirm 확인하다
- reconfirm 재확인하다

- **reservation** 예약
- **cancellation** 취소

- **take a tour** 관광 여행하다
- **museum** 박물관

⑪ AT AN AIRPORT (공항에서)

- **nationality** 국적
- **embarkation card** 출국 기록 카드
- **standby ticket** 대기자 티켓
- **customs office** 세관
- **boarding pass** 탑승권
- **baggage check** 수화물 보관증
- **duty** 관세
- **entry visa** 입국 비자
- **page** 호출하다(공항 등에서 스피커로)
- **boarding pass** 탑승

- **surname = family name** 성
- **disembarkation card** 입국 기록 카드
- **open ticket** 정해지지 않은 티켓(날짜, 시간)
- **customs Declaration Form** 세관 신고 용지
- **boarding gate** 탑승구
- **baggage claim area** 수화물 찾는 곳
- **duty-free shop** 면세점
- **entry permit** 입국 허가

⑫ IN THE PLANE (기내에서)

- **economy class** 일반석
- **business class** 비즈니스 석
- **window seat** 창문쪽 좌석
- **aisle seat** 통로쪽 좌석
- **flight attendant** 비행기 승무원
- **stewardess** 여자승무원
- **standard time** 표준시간
- **local time** 현지시간
- **flight time** 비행시간
- **time difference** 시차
- **bound for ~** ~행(行)

- **domestic flight** 국내선
- **overseas flight** 국제선
- **seat belt** 안전 벨트
- **fasten** 단단히 고정시키다
- **nonsmoking seat** 금연석
- **smoking seat** 끽연석
- **security check** 보안 검사대
- **quarantine desk** 검역대
- **available seats** 남은 좌석
- **be booked up** 예약이 마감되다
- **fill out** 기입하다

- **lay over = stop over** 중간 기항을 하다
- **beef or fish** 쇠고기 또는 생선
- **coffee or tea** 커피 또는 차

⑬ AT THE HOTEL (호텔에서)

- **reservation = booking** 예약

- **double occupancy** 2인 1실

- **make a reservation = reserve** 예약하다
- **check in** 입실하다
- **check out** 퇴실하다
- **closet** 벽장
- **suit** 특실
- **double room** 2인용 객실
- **fee** 수수료(의사, 변호사)

- **wake-up call = morning call** 깨워주는 전화
- **bill** (청구된) 요금
- **price** 물건 값
- **fare** 요금(운임)
- **single room** 1인용 객실
- **rate** 요금(호텔)
- **charge** 요금(전화, 전기등 청구)

⑭ SHOPPING (쇼핑)

- **shopping mall** 쇼핑 센터
- **department store** 백화점
- **bill** 지폐, 청구서
- **change** 거스름돈
- **quarter** 25센트
- **dime** 10센트
- **nickel** 5센트
- **check** 수표
- **cash** 현금
- **dozen** 12개
- **a couple of** 2개의
- **display** 진열, 진열하다
- **brand-new** 신상품의
- **secondhand** 중고품의
- **hand-made** 수제품의
- **products** 생산품
- **handout = leaflet** 광고 전단
- **product brochure** 제품 설명서
- **using slip** 사용 설명서
- **purchase** 구매, 구매하다
- **browse** 사지 않고 둘러보다
- **installment plan** 할부
- **lump sum** 일시불

- **convenience store** 편의점
- **vendor** 노점상, 자판기
- **vending machine** 자동판매기
- **shopping cart** 손님용 손수레
- **price tag** 가격표
- **receipt / sales slip** 영수증
- **wholesale price** 도매가
- **retail price** 소매가
- **clearance sale** 재고 정리 판매
- **half-price sale** 반액 할인 판매
- **closing-down sale** 폐업 세일
- **customer** 고객, 단골 손님
- **reasonable** 적당한
- **steep** 값비싼
- **regular price** 정가
- **take off = come down** 깍다
- **reduce = discount** 깍다
- **rise** 올리다
- **rip-off** 바가지
- **gratis** 무료 증정
- **refund** 환불
- **guarantee** 보증
- **gift-certificate** 상품권

- **How much is it? / How much do I cost?** 가격이 얼마입니까?
- **What's the price? / How much do I owe you?** 가격이 얼마입니까?

⑮ AT A HOSPITAL (병원에서)

- **general hospital** 종합병원
- **clinic** 개인(전문)의원
- **surgeon** 외과의사
- **physician** 내과의사
- **dentist** 치과의사
- **psychiatrist** 정신과의사
- **pediatrician** 소아과의사
- **pharmacist** 약사
- **prescription** 처방전
- **indigestion** 소화불량
- **high blood pressure** 고혈압
- **diabetes** 당뇨병
- **take a medicine** 약을 먹다

- **pneumonia** 폐렴
- **stomachache** 복통
- **toothache** 치통
- **flu** 독감
- **fever** 열
- **swollen** 부은
- **pale** 창백한
- **pregnant** 임신한
- **hoarse** 목이 쉰
- **tablet** (납작한)알약
- **pill** 알약
- **sneeze** 재채기하다
- **cough** 기침하다

- go to (the) hospital / be hospitalized 입원하다
- leave hospital 퇴원하다
- see a doctor 진찰받다
- I've caught a cold. 감기에 걸렸어요.
- I've a head cold. 두통 감기에 걸렸어요.
- I have a runny nose. 콧물이 나와요.
- I have a stuffy nose. 코가 막혔어요.
- I have a sore throat. 목이 아파요.
- I have a swollen tonsils. 편도선이 부었어요.
- I have a pain in my hand. 손에 통증이 있어요.
- He is down with the flu. 그는 독감으로 누워있어요.
- I have a touch of fever. 열이 좀 있어요.
- I've got a stiff shoulder. 어깨가 결립니다.
- I feel dizzy. 어지러워요.
- I'm allergic to pollen. 나는 꽃가루에 알레르기가 있어요.

⑯ WEATHER (날씨)

- **weather forecast** 일기예보
- **weatherman** 일기예보 아나운서
- **Celsius = centigrade** 섭씨

- **gale** 강풍
- **gust** 돌풍
- **tornado** 회오리바람

- **Fahrenheit** 화씨
- **high pressure** 고기압
- **low pressure** 저기압
- **chance of showers** 소나기 내릴 확률
- **rainstorm** 폭풍우
- **isolated showers** 곳에 따라 내리는 소나기
- **drizzle** 보슬비
- **downpour** 폭우
- **rainfall** 강우량
- **sleet** 진눈깨비
- **hail** 우박
- **breeze** 미풍

- **the highs** 최고 기온
- **the lows** 최저 기온
- **overcast** 잔뜩 흐린
- **foggy > misty > hazy** 안개 낀
- **muggy / humid** 후덥지근한
- **moist** (약간) 촉촉한
- **bleak** 살이 에는 듯한
- **chilly** 쌀쌀한
- **let up = stop** (비가) 그치다
- **dip down** (기온이) 내려가다
- **scorch** 푹푹 찌다
- **hold up** (날씨가) 계속되다

⑰ 자주 틀리기 쉬운 표현들

- **gas station** 주유소
- **flat tire** 펑크난 타이어
- **out of order** 고장난
- **fill it up** 기름을 가득 넣다

- **fix / repair** 고치다
- **reception** 접수처, 환영회
- **book** 예약하다
- **ball** 무도회

- I'll drop in later. 나중에 들르겠습니다.
- Put it on the scale. 그것을 저울에 올려놓으세요.
- Give me a hand. 도와 주십시오.
- I'll be there soon. 곧 가겠습니다.
- Let's break for ten minutes. 10분 쉽시다.
- I want to take off tomorrow. 내일 쉬고 싶습니다.
- Help yourself. 마음껏 드세요.

5. *Idiom Expression*(관용 표현)
관용 표현을 숙지해야 듣기가 된다.

[관용 표현 알아야 듣기가 된다
– 우리말로 쉽게 이해가 안되는 표현들]

1. I could use a day off. 하루 쉬었으면 좋겠습니다.
2. No way! That is way over my head. 제 머리로는 이해가 안되는군요.
3. I'll keep you posted. 당신에게 알려드릴 것이 있습니다.
4. Make mine the same. 저도 같은 걸로 주세요.
5. Which reminds me. 그러고 보니 생각이 나는군요.
6. I live in the country by choice. 제가 좋아서 시골에 삽니다.
7. Drop in any time you like. 좋으실 때 아무 때나 들르세요.
8. Stop bugging me. 괴롭히지 마.
9. Anything goes. 아무래도 좋습니다.
10. Don't play dumb. 어리석게 굴지 마.
11. Take care, Jessie. 잘 가, 제시.
12. It's against my nature. 그건 제 적성에 맞지 않습니다.
13. He's too forward. 그는 너무 나서기를 좋아해.
14. Watch your mouth. 말 조심해.
15. I owe you the truth. 너에게 사실대로 말할 게 있어.
16. Do I know you? 누구시더라?
17. Don't wear out your welcome. 일찍 돌아오너라.
18. Give it a thought. 생각 좀 해봐.
19. I couldn't agree more. 당신 말이 맞습니다.
20. What's eating you? 무슨 일이니?
21. Will it be soon(long)? 곧 됩니까? / 오래 걸립니까?
22. How do you want your steak? 스테이크를 어떻게 드릴까요?
23. Are you free this afternoon? 오후에 시간 있으세요?
24. I have a word with you. 당신에게 할 말이 있습니다.
25. Good job, Tom! 잘했어, 탐!
26. I'm a little lost. 약간 당황스럽군요.
27. It takes the cake! 단연 뛰어나군!
28. Get in. I'm going that way. 타, 나도 그 쪽 방향으로 가.

29. Where am I? 여기가 어딥니까?

30. My kids are crazy about Madonna. 저희 아이들은 마돈나를 너무나 좋아해요.

31. It's cinch. 누워서 떡 먹기야.

32. Do I look down in? 나 초라해 보이니?

33. Good for you. 잘 됐군요.

34. Think nothing of it. 그런건 잊어버리세요.

35. This picture flatters you. 사진이 실물보다 더 잘 나왔군요.

36. Let's go Dutch. 각자 부담합시다.

37. He drives me crazy. 그 사람 때문에 미치겠어.

38. Can I have a rain check? 다음 기회로 미루면 안될까요?

39. You're natural. 넌 타고났어.

40. She's a born shopper. 그녀는 정말 물건을 잘 사는군요.

41. May I propose a toast? 건배를 제의하겠습니다.

42. She's just in a jam. 그녀는 지금 어려움에 처해 있어.

43. I've had enough of this. 이젠 더 이상 못 참겠어.

44. Don't let me down. 꼭 약속을 지키세요.

45. You've missed the boat. 한 발 늦었습니다.

46. Take your best shot. 악착같이 해봐.

47. You are getting warm. 거의 온 것 같군. (스무 고개)

48. He hit the hay early. 그는 일찍 잠자리에 들었습니다.

49. What are you making a face for? 왜 얼굴을 찡그리고 있니?

50. You deserve it. 잘 됐군요.

51. Lighten up! 힘내세요!

52. It slipped my mind. 깜박 잊었습니다.

53. I can't tell you off hand. 지금 당장은 모르겠습니다.

54. I'm at my wit's end. 속수무책입니다.

55. God only knows. 아무도 모릅니다.

56. It's a real steal. 거의 공짜군요.

57. It made my day. 제 최고의 날이었습니다.

58. Serve you right! 꼴 좋군!

59. It's a disaster. 이거 낭패군.

60. Take your time. 서두르지 마세요.

61. You heard me wrong. 당신이 제 말을 오해하셨습니다.

62. Did you get the picture? 윤곽이 잡히세요?

63. I have no idea. 모르겠습니다.

64. Time sure flies. 세월이 유수와 같군요.

65. My back is killing me. 등이 아파 죽겠어요.

66. Don't be sure. 자만하지 마.

67. Everything is falling apart. 만사 끝장이야.

68. How can I put it in words? 그걸 어떻게 말로 하나요?

69. I love you beyond words. 너무나 당신을 사랑합니다.

70. He's a clock watcher. 그는 퇴근시간만 기다리는 사람이야.

71. I'm off today. 오늘은 쉬는 날입니다.

72. Let's call it a day. 이상 마칩시다.

73. That's the way he is. 그 친구 원래 그래.

74. That's my specialty. 그 일에는 내가 전문이지.

75. Don't mess it up! 망치지 마!

76. It works good. 일이 잘 풀리는군요.

77. What I earn is a chicken feed. 급여가 쥐꼬리만 합니다.

78. He wears two hats. 그는 두 가지 책임을 떠맡고 있습니다.

79. The hospital is two hours away. 그 병원은 2시간 거리입니다.

80. Calm down, boy. 이봐 진정해.

81. The bear is on the house. 맥주는 공짜야.

82. You look under the weather. 몸이 불편해 보이는군요.

83. I slept like a log. 푹 잤습니다.

84. It's on me. 내가 한턱 낼게.

85. Help me off. 이것 좀 벗겨 줘.

86. Something's coming up. 뭔가 일이 좀 생겼어.

87. That makes sense. 일리있군요.

88. You read my mind. 내가 하고 싶었던 말이야.

89. Same here. 나도 마찬가지야.

90. You can say that again. 전적으로 동감이야.

91. Nothing serious. 별거 아니야.

92. Let's set it over with. 빨리 끝냅시다.

93. The price is out of line. 너무 비싸군요.

94. Don't play boyscout with me. 시치미 떼지 마.

95. The traffic is bumper-to-bumper. 차들이 엄청나게 밀린다.

96. Would you give me a ride? 차 좀 태워 주실래요?

97. You get the picture? 이해가 됩니까?

98. That's not my dish. 저는 그런 것을 좋아하지 않습니다.

99. Same old stuff. 매 일 똑같군요.

100. Don't be freaked out. 화내지 마세요.

101. I didn't get steamed. 나는 화나지 않았어요.

102. Give me the details. 자세히 설명해 주세요.

103. End of the line. All disembark. 종점입니다. 내려주세요.

104. I always do first things first. 저는 늘 중요한 일을 먼저 합니다.

105. I only know her by sight. 저는 그 여자와 얼굴만 아는 정도입니다.

106. God, you're touching. 맙소사. 감동적이군.

107. This woman is made for you. 이 여자가 당산에게 맞는 상대입니다.

108. Things are heating up. -일이 점점 재미있어지는군요.

109. I screwed up. 일을 망쳤습니다.

110. She grows on you. 그 여자는 당신을 좋아하고 있습니다.

111. He knows his way around. 그는 사정을 훤히 알고 있습니다.

112. Let's have a ball. 자 마음껏 즐깁시다.

113. He has got the ball. 그는 칼자루를 쥔 사람이야.

114. He doesn't know the time of day. 그는 세상물정을 정말 모릅니다.

115. That can wait. 그건 나중에 해도 돼.

116. Am I clear? 제 말 알겠어요?

117. He has spoken out of turn. 그가 경솔하게 말했다.

118. I've been seeing her for two years. 나는 그녀와 2년간 사귀고 있습니다.

119. All right! Be that way! 그래! 마음대로 해 봐!

120. I thought as much. 그럴 것이라고 생각했습니다.

121. His song really gets to me every time. 그의 노래는 언제나 나의 심금을 울립니다.

122. Is this seat taken? 자리 비었습니까?

123. Am I bugging you? 제가 귀찮아요?

124. Go to it. 열심히 해 보세요.

125. I was not born yesterday. 저는 어린아이가 아닙니다.

126. That was all my fault. 모두 제 잘못이었습니다.

127. There's nothing that's easily done. 세상일이 쉬운 것이 없습니다.

128. He's a college dropout. 그는 대학 중퇴자입니다.

129. I'm at your disposal. 당신 처분대로 하겠습니다.

130. You know what? 알려드릴 것이 있습니다.

131. I'll come to that. 나중에 얘기하겠습니다.

132. You mean everything to me. 당신은 저에게 아주 소중한 사람입니다.

133. You bet. 물론입니다.

134. She's really too much. 그녀가 너무했습니다.

135. I heard you had a big day. 당신에게 좋은 일이 있다고 들었습니다.

136. No deal! 안됩니다.!

137. I couldn't be careless. 제가 간여할 일이 아닙니다.

138. Hang in there! 참고 견디세요!

139. Now you are talking! 그거 좋은 생각입니다!

Actual English Workbook

140. You're right on the money.   바로 맞추셨습니다.
141. Love is the name of the game.   사랑은 매우 중요한 일이지요.
142. Make no mistake about it.   착오없이 하세요.
143. I'm just thinking out loud.   단지 제 생각일 뿐입니다.
144. Don't get me wrong.   오해하지 마십시오.
145. I can't get it right.   잘 이해가 안됩니다.
146. I got back in one piece.   무사히 돌아왔습니다.
147. Just let your hair down.   편히 하십시오.
148. A really big deal happened.   정말 큰일났습니다.
149. She is walking on air.   그녀는 지금 의기양양합니다.
150. Let's go for it.   한 번 시도해 봅시다.
151. What a pity! 유감입니다.!
152. She stands tall.   그녀는 자신만만합니다.
153. She has it good.   그녀는 행운아입니다.
154. Disco is still going strong.   디스코 음악은 아직도 건재합니다.
155. Tell you what.   그럼 이렇게 합시다.
156. That figures.   그럴 줄 알았습니다.
157. You know better than that.   알만한 사람이 왜 그러십니까?
158. Catch you later at the cafeteria.   식당에서 봅시다.
159. Beats me.   전혀 모르겠군.
160. My kids come first.   제 자식들 말고 누구겠어요.
161. Boy, that's a beer.   맥주 맛 좋다!
162. That can wait.   그건 나중에 해도 돼.
163. Do your homework.   사전에 준비하세요.
164. There is no free lunch.   세상에 공짜가 없습니다.
165. Well, that's that.   이제 다 끝났습니다.
166. You sure wear many hats.   당신은 여러 가지를 할 줄 아는군요.
167. You got it. I'll be right.   알았습니다. 금방 다녀오겠습니다.
168. The jury's still out on that issue.   그 쟁점은 아직도 결말을 보지 못하고 있습니다.
169. She's got what it takes to be a signer.   그녀는 가수가 될 소질이 있습니다.
170. He knows his way around.   그는 사정을 훤히 알고 있습니다.
171. I feel lke a new person.   날아갈 것 같은 기분입니다.
172. Easy does it. Easy does it.   조심조심 천천히 하세요.
173. She's got it made.   그녀는 떼놓은 당상입니다.
174. He's playing hardball.   그녀는 강경한 태도를 보이고 있습니다.
175. She's on top of the current English.   그녀는 시사영어에 능통합니다.
176. We'll have to cut corners.   경비를 절감해야겠어요.

177. I don't want to name names. 누구라고 밝히고 싶지 않습니다.

178. Let's just play it by ear. 봐서 결정합시다.

179. Don't rock the boat. 평지풍파를 일으키지 마세요.

180. That's interesting? 그래요?

181. I'm telling you. 제 말을 잘 들으세요.

182. Leave me alone. 내버려 두세요.

183. He's a pretty tough cookie. 그는 만만치 않은 사람입니다.

184. I'm up to my ears in work. 일 때문에 꼼짝 못하겠어요.

185. You've come a long way. 장족의 발전을 하셨군요.

186. I lost my shirt. 큰 돈을 잃었습니다.

187. Life is like that. 인생이란 다 그런 것이지요.

188. She has come into her own. 그녀의 진가가 드러났습니다.

189. I'll just come in cold. 준비없이 그냥 들어가겠습니다.

190. Are you through with that paper? 신문 다 읽으셨습니까?

191. No soft soap for me. 비행기 태우지 마세요.

192. Can you break a hundred dollar bill? 100달러짜리 지폐를 바꿔줄 수 있으세요?

193. Business is picking up. 사업이 호전되고 있습니다.

194. Pull over! 차를 저기다 세우세요.

195. Stop bossing me around! 이래라 저래라 하지 마세요!

196. How come you're so observing? 왜 그렇게 관심이 많으세요.

197. Do you have a college experience? 대학에 다녀본 적이 있습니까?

198. I think I'm lost. 길을 잃었습니다.

199. May I have a barf bag, please? 구토용 봉투 좀 주세요.

200. How long are you going to be away? 얼마나 오래 있을 예정입니까?

201. Kids are building a snowman. 아이들이 눈사람을 만들고 있습니다.

202. I've got nothing to wear. 입을 옷이 하나도 없습니다.

203. She's good at drawing. 그녀는 그림을 잘 그립니다.

204. Stop the thief! 도둑 잡아라!

205. Do you carry dog food? 개밥 있습니까?

206. When is the baby due? 출산 예정일은 언제입니까?

207. She is expecting. 그녀는 임신 중입니다.

208. Please call me first thing in the morning. 내일 아침 일찍 전화 주세요.

209. May I be excused? 잠시 실례해도 되겠습니까?

210. Let this be a lesson to you. 이것을 교훈으로 삼으세요.

211. (Is) My presence here annoying you? 제가 있어서 거북한 것 아닙니까?

212. He's in a fog. 그는 완전히 취했습니다.

213. You'd better keep it. 모아 두는 것이 좋겠군요.

214. Thank you for the ride.   차를 태워 줘서 고마워요.

215. Do you have any vacanies?   빈 방이 있습니까?

216. Money doesn't go too far.   별로 살 것이 없군요.

217. Are you decent?   들어가도 됩니까?

218. How much do I owe you?   얼마입니까?

219. Are you seeing anyone?   사귀는 사람이 있으세요?

220. Put your cigarette out.   담배 불 좀 꺼주세요.

221. Is there any job opening?   취업할 자리가 있습니까?

222. The position has been filled.   자리가 없습니다.

223. You've got to share!   함께 가지고 놀아가!

224. Now, just hold your horses and let me explain.   천천히 내 말 좀 들어보세요.

225. That won't work.   고장입니다.

226. Do you want some giggle?   재미있는 이야기를 해 줄까요?

227. I want to get even with him.   그에게 꼭 앙갚음을 하겠어.

228. We're having a field day tomorrow.   내일 운동회가 있습니다.

229. She's a sloppy dresser.   그녀는 옷을 깔끔하게 입지 못합니다.

230. Did I get any calls?   제게 전화 온 것이 있습니까?

231. She hit me where I hurt most.   그녀는 제가 아파하는 곳을 찔렀다.

232. It hurts like the devil.   지독하게 아프군요.

233. He's hogging the phone.   저 친구 전화를 너무 오래 쓰는군.

234. Nice anything different about me?   나 어디 달라진 것 없어요?

235. Couldn't be better.   아주 좋습니다.

236. She has a soft spot for animals.   그녀는 동물애호가입니다.

237. He's going to be somebody someday.   그는 언젠가는 훌륭한 사람이 될 거예요.

238. We took a spell at the wheel.   우리는 교대로 운전했습니다.

239. I'm on pins and needles.   나는 바늘방석에 앉아 있습니다.

240. The game was rained out.   그 경기는 바로 취소되었습니다.

241. I'm just a phone call away.   전화만 주시면 언제든 갈 수 있습니다.

242. Let's call a spade a spade.   솔직하게 말합시다.

243. He's still carrying on.   그는 아직도 바람을 피우고 있습니다.

244. Will that be cash, or charge?   현금으로 하시겠습니까? 카드로 하시겠습니까?

245. That's short notice!   그렇게 갑자기 말하면 어떻게 합니까!

246. I've lost 5 pounds. Does it show?   5파운드 줄인 것으로 보여요?

247. Whose side are you on? 당신은 누구 편입니까?

248. Are you still sore at me?   아직도 제게 화가 나 있습니까?

249. Slow down. Do not tailgate.   천천히 가십시오. 앞차에 너무 붙지 마세요.

250. Korea might win it, but it won't be a tea party.   한국이 쉽게 이길 것 같지 않군요.

251. Are you up? 자니?

252. I think I can use a cup of coffee. 커피 한 잔 해야겠어요.

253. Why don't you warm it up? It got cold. 따뜻한 물 더 드릴까요?

254. That's some stuff! 대단하군!

255. My foot went to sleep. 다리가 저립니다.

256. He's down to earth. 그는 현실적인 사람이야.

257. I wonder who the lucky person is! 행운의 사나이가 누구지?

258. Hit the books hard. 공부 열심히 하세요.

259. Hold my place. I'll be right back. 자리 좀 봐주세요. 금방 오겠습니다.

260. He slept through the incident. 그는 세상 모르고 자고 있었다.

261. That's a shame! 저런 참 안됐군요.

262. Step on the gas! 서둘러 주세요!

263. My refrigerator is on the blink. 냉장고가 시원치 않습니다.

264. Are you all by yourself? 너 혼자 있니?

265. They're poles apart. 그들은 극과 극이다.

266. Who do you bank with? 어느 은행과 거래하십니까?

267. It's like biting the hand that feeds. 배은망덕하군.

268. Don't blow it! 실수 없이 잘 하세요!

269. Our time is running. Please boil it down. 시간이 다 되었으니 요약해 주세요.

270. You'd better come clean. 다 털어 놓으세요.

271. I think I'm coming down with cold. 아무래도 감기가 오는 것 같다.

272. Come on! I'll pop. I'm loaded. 갑시다. 제가 한턱 내겠습니다.

273. He called in sick. 그는 아프다고 전화 왔습니다.

274. Go easy on the drink. 술 조금만 마십시오.

275. You guys feel like some dinner. 저녁 먹을래?

276. Let's give him a big hand. 그에게 큰 박수를 보냅시다.

278. I hate to see you go. 당신이 가지 않았으면 좋겠습니다.

279. She's a home-body. 그는 집에만 있는 사람입니다.

280. Straight home from school! 학교 마치고 곧장 와.

281. That's that. 그것으로 다 끝났습니다.

282. You have a point there. 당신 말에도 일리가 있습니다.

283. Can you make it? 할 수 있겠습니까?

284. You know better than that. 알만한 사람이 왜 그러십니까?

285. Am I welcome? 제가 못 올 곳에 왔습니까?

286. Freeze! 꼼짝 마!

287. I'm tired of watching T.V. 텔레비전 보는 것도 지겹습니다.

DAYS, MONTHS, NUMBERS

■ DAYS OF THE WEEK

Sunday, Monday, Tuesday, Wednesday, Thursday, Friday, Saturday

■ MONTHS OF THE YEAR

January, February, March, April, May, June, July, August, September, October, November, December

■ NUMBERS

1	one	101	a hundred and one	1st	first
2	two	102	a hundred and two	2nd	second
3	three	160	a hundred and sixty	3rd	third
4	four	200	two hundred	4th	fourth
5	five	301	three hundred and one	5th	fifth
6	six	484	four hundred and eighty-four	6th	sixth
7	seven	1,000	a / one thousand	7th	seventh
8	eight	3,856	three thousand eight hundred and fifty-six	8th	eighth
9	nine			9th	ninth
10	ten			10th	tenth
11	eleven			11th	eleventh
12	twelve			12th	twelfth
13	thirteen			13th	thirteenth
14	fourteen			14th	fourteenth
15	fifteen			15th	fifteenth
16	sixteen			16th	sixteenth
17	seventeen			17th	seventeenth
18	eighteen			18th	eighteenth
19	nineteen			19th	nineteenth
20	twenty			20th	twentieth
21	twenty-one			21st	twenty-first
22	twenty-two			22nd	twenty-second
30	thirty			30th	thirtieth
40	forty			40th	fortieth
50	fifty			50th	fiftieth
60	sixty			60th	sixtieth
70	seventy			70th	seventieth
80	eighty			80th	eightieth
90	ninety			90th	ninetieth
100	a / one hundred			100th	hundredth

6. Useful Expression (유용한 표현)

유용한 일상표현을 암기해야 회화가 된다.

UNIT 1 GREETINGS (인사하기)

1 Hello.	2 Good morning.
3 I'm John Smith.	4 Are you Bill Jones?
5 Yes, I am.	6 How are you?
7 Fine, thanks.	8 How is Helen?
9 She's very well, thank you.	
10 Good afternoon, Mr. Green.	
11 Good evening, Mrs. Brown.	
12 How are you this evening?	
13 Good night, John.	
14 Good-bye, Bill.	
15 See you tomorrow.	

UNIT 2 CLASSROOM EXPRESSIONS (강의실 표현)

16 Come in, please.

17 Sit down.

18 Stand up, please.

19 Open your book please.

20 Close your book, please.

21 Don't open your book.

22 Do you understand?

23 Yes, I understand.

24 No, I don't understand.

25 Listen and repeat.

26 Now read, please.

27 That's fine.

28 It's time to begin.

29 Let's begin now.

30 This is Lesson One.

UNIT 3 IDENTIFYING OBJECTS (물건의 구별과 소유)

31 What's this?

32 That's book.

33 Is this your book?

34 No, that's not my book.

35 Whose book is this?

36 That's your book.

37 And what's that?

38 Is that a book?

39 No, it isn't.

40 It's a pencil.

41 Is it yours?

42 Yes, it's mine.

43 Where's the door?

44 There it is.

45 Is this book his?

UNIT 4 IDENTIFYING OBJECTS (물건의 구별과 위치)

46 What are these?

47 Those are books.

48 Where are the books?

49 There they are.

50 There are my pencils.

51 Where are your pens?

52 They're over there.

53 Are these your pens?

54 Yes, there are.

55 Those are mine.

56 There are your books, aren't they?

57 No, they aren't.

58 They're not mine.

59 There are mine, and those are yours.

60 Those aren' t your pens. are they?

UNIT **5** IDENTIFYING PEOPLE BY OCCUPATION (사람과 직업 확인)

61 Who are you?

62 I'm a student.

63 Who is that over there?

64 He's a student, too.

65 Is that lady a student?

66 No, she isn't.

67 Those men aren't students, either.

68 Am I your teacher?

69 Yes, you are.

70 That man is a teacher, isn't he?

71 Yes, he is.

72 Who are those people?

73 Maybe they're farmers.

74 Aren't they students?

75 I really don't know.

UNIT **6** INTRODUCTIONS AND COURTESIES (소개와 예절)

76 What's your name?

77 My name is Jones.

78 What's your first name?

79 My first name is Bill.

80 How do you spell your last name?

81 Jones. J-O-N-E-S.

82 What's your friend's name?

83 His name is John Smith.

84 John and I are old friends.

85 Are you John's brother?

86 No, I'm not.

87 This is Mr. Jones.

88 How do you do?

89 Mrs. Jones, this is Mr. John Smith.

90 Very pleased to meet you.

UNIT 7 DAYS AND MONTHS OF THE CALENDAR (요일 표현)

91 What day is today?

92 Today is Monday.

93 What day was yesterday?

94 Yesterday was Sunday.

95 What day is tomorrow?

96 What month is this?

97 This is January.

98 Last mont was December, wasn't it?

99 Yes, it was.

100 What months is next month?

101 I was in the hospital for several weeks.

102 Where were you on Tuesday?

103 You were here in February, weren't you?

104 No, I wasn't.

105 Your friend was here a week ago, wasn't he?

UNIT 8 TALKING ABOUT OBJECTS (물건 소유와 색체 표현)

106 Do you have a book?

107 Yes, I do.

108 You have a radio, don't you?

109 No, I don't.

110 I don't have a phonograph, either.

111 Does this radio belong to you?

112 Yes, I think it does.

113 How many sisters and brothers do you have?

114 Don't you have my hat?

115 Yes, I have both your hat and your coat.

116 Does John have a yellow pencil?

117 Yes, he does.

118 He has a radio, doesn't he?

119 No, he doesn't have one.

120 He already has a phonograph, but he doesn't have a radio yet.

UNIT **9** TELLING TIME (시간 묻기)

121 What time is it?

122 It's two o'clock.

123 It's a few minutes after two.

124 My watch is fast and your watch is slow.

125 Excuse me. Can you tell me the correct time?

126 No, I can't.

127 I don't know what time it is.

128 I don't think it's four o'clock yet.

129 It must be about three thirty.

130 I get up before six o'clock every day.

131 The restaurant doesn't open until seven forty-five.

132 Will you be here at ten o'clock tomorrow?

133 Yes, I will.

134 We'll be on time, won't we?

135 I hope so.

UNIT **10** TALKING ABOUT DATES (날짜 표현)

136 What's the date today?

137 Today is November first, nineteen sixty-three.

138 When were you born?

139 I was born on November first, nineteen thirty-five.

140 Today is my birthday.

141 My sister was born in nineteen thirty-eight.

142 I don't know the exact date.

143 Where were you born?

144 I was born in a little town not far from here.

145 What do you know about the tenth century?

146 I don't know anything about that.

147 Let's talk about something else.

148 Where were you during the month of April last year?

149 I don't remember where I was then.

150 Where will you be next year at this time?

UNIT **11** TALKING ABOUT OBJECTS AND PEOPLE (권유하기, 용모에 관하여)

151 What do you want?

152 I want a cup of coffee.

153 What would you like to eat?

154 Please give me a piece of pie.

155 Which one would you like - this one or that one?

156 It doesn't matter to me.

157 I'd like to talk with Mr. Jones or Mr. Smith.

158 I'm sorry, but both of them are busy right now.

159 Wouldn't you like some coffee?

160 I'd rather have some tea, if you don't mind.

161 Do you know any of those people?

162 Two or three of them look familiar.

163 All of those people are friends of mine.

164 Which one of those men is Mr. Taylor?

165 Is he the tall man on the left?

UNIT **12** TALKING ABOUT LANGUAGES (언어, 외국어 표현)

166 Do you speak English?

167 Yes, a little.

168 Does your friend speak English?

169 Yes, he speaks English perfectly.

170 What's his native language?

171 I don't know what his native language is.

172 How many languages do you speak?

173 My friend reads and writes several languages.

174 How well do you know French?

175 He speaks French with an American accent.

176 My parents speak English flently.

177 Mr. Jones can read French pretty well.

178 Sometimes I make mistakes when I speak English.

179 I have a lot of trouble with pronunciation.

180 How is her accent in French?

UNIT **13** TALKING ABOUT ACTIVITIES (일상의 활동)

181　What are you doing?

182　I'm reading a book?

183　What's your friend doing?

184　He's studying his lesson.

185　I'm not doing anything right now.

186　Where are you going?

187　I'm going home.

188　What tim are you coming back?

189　I'm not sure what time I'm coming back.

190　What are you thinking about?

191　I'm thinking about my lesson.

192　Who are you writing to?

193　I'm writing to a friend of mine in South America.

194　By the way, who are you waiting for?

195　I'm not waiting for anybody.

UNIT **14** ASKING ABOUT AGE (나이 묻고, 대답하기)

196　How old are you?

197　I'm twenty-one years old.

198　My brother is not quite twenty-five.

199　John is not forty-five yet, is he?

200　Mr. Smith is still in his fifties.

201　I'm two years older than you are.

202　My brother is two years younger than I am.

203　How many are there in your family?

204　There are seven of us altogether.

205　My sister is the oldest.

206　I'm the youngest.

207　Guess how old I am.

208　I'd say you're about twenty-three.

209　I was thirty on my last birthday.

210　I'm going to be sixty-one next Tuesday.

UNIT 15 TALKING ABOUT DAILY ACTIVITIES (일상생활에 관한 대화)

211 What time do you get up every day?

212 I usually wake up early.

213 I get up at 6 o'clock every day.

214 My brother gets up later than I do.

215 After I get dressed, I have breakfast.

216 Usually, I have a big breakfast.

217 I have juice, cereal, toast, and coffee for breakfast.

218 I leave the house at eight a.m. each day.

219 I get to work at nine o'clock every morning.

220 I work hard all morning.

221 I go out for lunch at about 12:30.

222 I finish working at 5:45 p.m.

223 I eat dinner at about 7 o'clock.

224 Before I eat dinner, I read the newspaper for a while.

225 I usually go to bed at about midnight.

UNIT 16 TALKING ABOUT YESTERDAY'S ACTIVITIES (과거의 일−1)

226 What time did you get up yesterday morning?

227 I woke up early and got up at 6 o'clock.

228 My brother got up earlier than I did.

229 Did you get dressed right away?

230 Yes, I got dressed and had breakfast.

231 What kind of breakfast did you have?

232 What time did you get to work yesterday morning?

233 I left the house at 8 o'clock and got to work at 8:30.

234 Did you work all day?

235 Yes, I worked from early morning until late at night.

236 At noon I had lunch with a friend of mine.

237 I finished working at 5:30 and went home.

238 After dinner I read a magazine and made some telephone calls.

239 I went to bed at 11:30 p.m.

240 I went to sleep immediately and slept soundly all night.

UNIT 17 MEETING A FRIEND (친구 만나기)

241 Where did you go yester?

242 I went to see a friend of mine.

243 Did you see Mr. Jones yesterday?

244 I didn't see Mr. Jones, but I saw John Smith.

245 What did you talk about?

246 We talked about a lot of things.

247 I asked him a lot of questions.

248 What did you ask him?

249 I asked him if he spoke Engligh.

250 He said he spoke a little English.

251 Then I asked him if he knew anybody in New York.

252 He said he knew a lot of people there.

253 Finally, I asked him how old he was.

254 He said he would rather not tell his age.

255 He answered almost all of my questions.

UNIT 18 TALKING ABOUT LAST YEAR'S ACTIVITIES (과거의 일-2)

256 What time did you use to get up last year?

257 I used to wake up early and get up at 7 o'clock.

258 I used to set my alarm clock for exactly 7 a.m.

259 I never used to oversleep.

260 I used to get dressed quickly every morning.

261 I always used to leave for work at 8:30.

262 I used to start working at 9:00 o'clock every day.

263 I used to have lunch every day at the same time.

264 I used to work until nearly 6:00 o'clock each day.

265 I used to have dinner at 7:30 and go to bed early.

266 My brother and I used to go a lot of places together.

267 We used to go to the movies about once a week.

268 We used to have a lot of interesting friends.

269 My brother used to speak Frenc to me all the time.

270 I always used to ask him a lot of questions.

UNIT 19 ASKING ABOUT ADDRESSES (주소 묻기)

271 Where do you live?

272 I live on Washington Street.

273 What's your address?

274 I live at 1203 Washington Street.

275 I'm Mr. Smith's next door neighbor.

276 You live here in the city, don't you?

277 I'm from out of town.

278 How long have you lived here?

279 I've lived here for five years.

280 He's known me for over ten years.

281 I've spoken English all my life.

282 I've already read that book.

283 Has he studied Frenc very long?

284 Have you had breakfast already?

285 Yes, I had breakfast two hours ago.

UNIT 20 ASKING QUESTIONS (질문하기)

286 Where were you yesterday afternoon?

287 I was at home all afternoon.

288 I was writing some letters to friends of mine.

289 What were you doing at about 4 o'clock yesterday afternoon.

290 I was listening to the radio.

291 What were you doing When I called you on the telephone?

292 When you called me, I was eating dinner.

293 When I saw Mr. Jones, he was talking with John Smith.

294 While you were writing letters, I was reading a book.

295 While we were having breakfast, John was talking on the telephone.

296 Can you guess what I was doing this morning?

297 I can't remember what John was doing yesterday afternoon.

298 I've forgotten what he said his address was.

299 I've forgotten what time he said he had dinner last night.

300 They called us just as we were having dinner.

UNIT 21 DESCRIBING OBJECTS (특징 묘사하기)

301 What color is your book?

302 My book has a dark blue cover.

303 How much does that typewriter weight?

304 It's not too heavy, but I don't know the exact weight.

305 This round table weighs about forty-five pounds.

306 What size suicase do you won?

307 One of my suitcases is small, and the other one is medium size.

308 I like the shape of that table.

309 How long is Jones Boulevard?

310 That street is only two miles long.

311 Will you please measure this window to see how wide it is?

312 This window is just as wide as that one.

313 The walls are three inches thick.

314 This material feels soft.

315 This pencil is longer than that one.

UNIT 22 ASKING PEOPLE TO DO THINGS (부탁할 때)

316 Would you please tell Mr. Cooper that I'm here?

317 Take these books home with you tonight.

318 Please bring me those magazines.

319 Would you help me lift this heavy box?

320 Please ask John to turn on the lights.

321 Put your books down on the table.

322 Get me a hammer from the kitchen, will you?

323 Hang up my coat in the closet, will you please?

324 Please don't bother me now. I'm very busy.

325 Would you mind mailing this letter for me?

326 If you have time, will you call me tomorrow?

327 Please pick up those cups and saucers.

328 Will you do me a favor?

329 Please count the chairs in that room.

330 Please pour this milk into that glass.

UNIT 23 GETTING INFORMATION AND DIRECTIONS (길에서 방향 묻기)

331 Excuse me, sir. Can you give me some information?

332 Can you tell me where Peach Street is?

333 It's two blocks straight ahead.

334 Which direction is it to the theater?

335 Turn right at the next corner.

336 How far is it to the university?

337 It's long way from here.

338 The school is just around the corner.

339 The restaurant is across the street from the hotel.

340 You can't miss it.

341 Do you happen to know Mr. Cooper's telephone number?

342 Could you tell me where the nearest telephone is?

343 Should I go this way, or that way?

344 Go that way for two blocks, then turn left?

345 I beg your pardon. Is this seat taken?

UNIT 24 TALKING ABOUT FAMILY AND RELATIVES (결혼과 일가 친척)

346 Are you married?

347 No, I'm not married. I'm still single.

348 Your niece is engaged, isn't she?

349 My sister has been engaged for two months.

350 My grandfather got married in 1921.

351 When is your grandparents' wedding anniversary?

352 How long have they been married?

353 They've been married for quite a few years.

354 Who did George marry?

355 Do they have children?

356 They had a baby last month.

357 My son wants to get married in June.

358 They don't know when the wedding will he.

359 Their grandchildren are grown up now.

360 She's a widow. Her husband died last year.

UNIT 25 TALKING ABOUT NEIGHBORS AND FRIENDS (이웃과 친구)

361 Where did you grow up?

362 I grew up right here in this neighborhood.

363 My friend spent his childhood in California.

364 He lived in California until he was seventeen.

365 There have been a lot of changes here in the last 20 years.

366 There used to be a grocery store on the corner

367 All of those houses have been built in the last ten years.

368 They're building a new house up the street from me.

369 If you buy that home, will you spend the rest of your life there?

370 Are your neighbors very friendly?

371 We all know each other pretty well.

372 A young married couple moved in next door to us.

373 Who bought that new house down the street from you?

374 An elderly man rented the big white house.

375 What beautiful trees those are!

UNIT 26 TALKING ABOUT FUTURE ACTIVITIES (미래의 일-1)

376 What time are you going to get up tomorrow morning?

377 I'll probably wake up early and get up at 6:30.

378 What will you do then?

379 After I get dressed, I'll have breakfast.

380 What will you have for breakfast tomorrow morning?

381 I'll probably have eggs and toast for breakfast.

382 After breakfast, I'll get ready to go to work.

383 I'll leave the house at 8:00 and get to the office at 8:30.

384 I'll probably go out for lunch at about 12:30.

385 I'll finish working at 5:30 and get home by 6 o'clock.

386 Are you going to have dinner at home tomorrow night?

387 Do you think you'll go to the movies tomorrow night?

388 I'll probably stay home and watch television.

389 When I get sleepy, I'll probably get ready for bed.

390 Do you think you'll be able to go to sleep right away?

UNIT **27** TALKING ABOUT THE WEATHER (날씨 표현)

391 How is the weather today?
392 The weather is nice today.
393 What was the weather like yesterday?
394 Yesterday it rained all day.
395 What will the weather be like tomorrow?
396 It's going to snow tomorrow.
397 It's quite cold today.
398 It's been cloudy all morning.
399 Is it raining now?
400 It'll probably clear up this afternoon.
401 The days are getting hotter.
402 Today is the first day of spring.
403 What's the temperature today?
404 It's about seventy degrees Fahrenheit this afternoon.
405 There's a cool breeze this evening.

UNIT **28** TALKING ABOUT SICKNESS AND HEALTH (질병과 건강)

406 How are you feeling today?
407 I don't feel very well this morning.
408 I was sick yesterday, but I'm better today.
409 My fever is gone, but I still have a cough.
410 My brother has a bad headache.
411 Which of your arms is sore?
412 My right arm hurts. It hurts right here.
413 What's the matter with you?
414 I've got a pain in my back.
415 Which foot hurts? Is it the left one?
416 How did you break your leg?
417 I slipped on the stairs and fell down. I broke my leg.
418 Your right hand is swollen. Does it hurt?
419 It's bleeding. You'd better go see a doctor about that cut.
420 I hoe you'll be well soon.

UNIT 29 TALKING ABOUT DAILY HABITS (일상의 습관)

421 I get out of bed about 7 o'clock every morning.

422 After getting up, I go into the bathroom and take a shower.

423 Then, I shave, brush my teeth and comb my hair.

424 After brushing my teeth, I put on my clothes.

425 After that, I go downstairs to the kitchen to have breakfast.

426 After eating breakfast, I go back upstairs again.

427 Then, it's usually time to wake up my little brother.

428 He can't dress himself yet because he's too young.

429 I wash his face and hands, and then I dress him.

430 He tries to button his own shirt, but he can't do it.

431 My little brother takes a bath before he goes to bed at night.

432 He always forgets to wash behind his ears.

433 I'm always tired when I come home from work.

434 At bedtime, I take off my clothes and put on my pajamas.

435 I get into bed at about 11:30, and go right off to sleep.

UNIT 30 GETTING OTHER PEOPLE'S OPINIONS AND IDEAS (의견과 아이디어)

436 What do you think? Is that right?

437 Certainly. You're absolutely right about that.

438 I think you're mistaken about that.

439 I like hot weather best.

440 Personally, I prefer winter weather.

441 Do you think it's going to rain tomorrow?

442 I don't know whether it will rain or not.

443 In my opinion, that's an excellent idea.

444 Why is Mr. Cooper so tired? Do you have any idea?

445 He's tired because he worked hard all day today.

446 What do you think of my children?

447 I think you have very attractive children.

448 Please give me your frank opinion.

449 Do you really want to know what I think?

450 Of course I want to know what your opinion is!

UNIT 31 MAKING PLANS (계획 세우기)

451 What do you plan to do tomorrow?

452 I doubt that I'll do anything tomorrow.

453 Please excuse me for a little while. I want to do something.

454 I imagine I'll do some work instead of going to the movies.

455 Will it be convenient for you to explain your plans to him?

456 There's nothing to do because tomorrow is a holiday.

457 What's your brother planning to do tomorrow?

458 He can't decide what to do.

459 It's difficult to make a decision without knowing all the facts.

460 We're trying to plan our future.

461 That's good idea.

462 I'm hoping to spend a few days in the mountains.

463 Would you consider going north this summer?

464 If there's a chance you'll go, I'd like to go with you.

465 After you think it over, please let me know what you decide.

UNIT 32 MAKING DECISIONS (결정하기)

466 I'm anxious to know what your decision is.

467 I'm confident you've made the right choice.

468 I want to persuade you to change your mind.

469 Will you accept my advice?

470 What have you decided?

471 I've definitely decided to go to California.

472 He didn't want to say anything to influence my decision.

473 She refuses to make up her mind.

474 I assume you've decided against buying a new car.

475 It took him a long time to make up his mind.

476 You can to whenever you wish.

477 We're willing to accept your plan.

478 He know it's inconvenient, but he wants to go anyway.

479 According to Mr. Green, this is a complicated problem.

480 She insists that it doesn't make any difference to her.

UNIT **33** GOING PLACES (여행에 관한 대화)

481 Are you going to go anyplace this year?

482 If I have enough money, I'm going to take a trip abroad.

483 How are you going? Are you going by boat?

484 It's faster to go by plane than by boat.

485 What's the quickest way to get there?

486 Altogether it will take ten days to make the trip.

487 I hope you have a good time on your trip.

488 I'm leaving tomorrow, but I haven't packed my suitcases yet.

489 I'm going by air. I like flying.

490 My brother took a trip to Mexico.

491 It was a six-hour flight.

492 How many passengers were on the train?

493 His friend was injured in an airplane crash.

494 Would you lik to go for a walk?

495 Let's go out to the airport. The plane landed ten minutes ago.

UNIT **34** GOING SHOPPING (물건 사기)

496 I'm going shopping because I need to buy some clothes.

497 If this shirt doesn't fit, may I bring it back later?

498 What size shoes do you wear?

499 That suit looks very good on you.

500 This dress is made of silk, isn't it?

501 I'd like to try on this sweater.

502 I'm interested in buying a new car.

503 What's the price of that electric iron?

504 How much is this rug?

505 Is this toothpaste on sale today?

506 That's a beautiful leather wallet, but it costs too much.

507 How much do I owe you?

508 That will be eighteen dollars and seventy-five cents.

509 Do you have change for a twenty-dollar bill?

510 The clerk helped me find what I wanted.

UNIT **35** EATING IN A RESTAURANT (음식과 식당)

511 What would you like to eat?

512 I'd like a bowl of tomato soup, please.

513 The waiter seems to be in a hurry to take our order.

514 Which would you rather have - steak or fish?

515 I want my steak well-done.

516 What kinds of vegetables do you have?

517 I'll have mashed potatoes and green beans.

518 Would you please pass the salt?

519 They serve good food in this restaurant.

520 Are you ready for your dessert now?

521 This knife is dirty. Would you bring me a clean one, please?

522 May I have the check, please?

523 You have your choice of three flavors of ice cream.

524 We have vanilla, chocolate, and strawberry.

525 We invited two guests to dinner, but they didn' t come.

UNIT **36** GOING OUT FOR THE EVENING (저녁 나들이)

526 How long did the movie last?

527 The feature started at 9 o'clock and ended at 11:30.

528 They say the new film is an adventure story.

529 A group of us went out to the theater last night.

530 The new play was good and everybody enjoyed it.

531 By the time we got there, the play had already begun.

532 The usher showed us to our seats.

533 The cast of the play included a famous actor.

534 After the play was over, we all wanted to get something to eat.

535 There was a big crowd and we had difficulty getting a taxi.

536 The restaurant was filled, so we decided to go elsewhere.

537 My brother wants to learn how to dance.

538 We don't go dancing very often.

539 Which would you rather do - go dancing or go to a play?

540 I'm not accustomed to going out after dark.

UNIT 37 MAKING APPOINTMENTS (약속하기)

541 I'd like to make an appointment to see Mr. Cooper.

542 Would you like to arrange for a personal interview?

543 Your appointment will be next Thursday at 10 o'clock.

544 I can come any day except Thursday.

545 He wants to change his appointment from Monday to Wednesday.

546 She failed to call the office to cancel her appointment.

547 I'm going to call the employment agency for a job.

548 Pleas fill in this application form.

549 Are you looking for a permanent position?

550 I'm going to call a plumber to come this afternoon.

551 I couldn't keep the appointment because I was sick.

552 I'm a new employee, I was hired yesterday.

553 Please call before you come, otherwise we might not be home.

554 Let's make a date to go shopping next Thursday.

555 Will you please lock the door when you leave?

UNIT 38 VISITING THE DOCTOR (병원 가기)

556 I went to see my doctor for a check-up yesterday.

557 The doctor discovered that I'm a little overweight.

558 He gave me a chest X-ray and took my blood pressure.

559 He told me to take these pills every four hours.

560 Do you think the patient can be cured?

561 They operated on him last night.

562 He needed a blood transfusion.

563 My uncle had a heart attack last year.

564 They had to call in a heart specialist.

565 What did the doctor say?

566 The doctor advised me to get plenty of exercise.

567 The doctor said I look pale.

568 If I want to be healthy, I have to stop smoking cigarettes.

569 The physician said smoking is harmful to my health.

570 It's just a mosquito bite. There's nothing to worry about.

UNIT 39 MAKING TELEPHONE CALLS (전화 걸기)

571 You're wanted on the telephone.

572 What number should I dial to get the operator?

573 I want to make a long distance call.

574 Pick up the receiver and deposit a coin in the slot.

575 I tried to call Mr. Cooper, but the line was busy.

576 You must have dialed the wrong number.

577 I dialed the right number, but nobody answered.

578 The telephone is ringing. Would you answer it, please?

579 Would you like to leave a message?

580 Who is this? I don't recognize your voice.

581 Would you please tell Mr. Cooper I called?

582 Is this Empire 5-4093?

583 I have a hang up now.

584 Put the receiver closer to your mouth. I can't hear you.

585 Would you mind calling back sometime tomorrow?

UNIT 40 WRITING LETTERS (편지 쓰기)

586 How long has it been since you've heard from your uncle?

587 When was the last time he wrote you?

588 I can't recall how long it's been.

589 I'm always disappointed when I don't get any mail.

590 I feel guilty because I haven't written her lately.

591 What time is the mail delivered on Saturday?

592 The postman always comes at 2 o'clock.

593 I wrote to my uncle last night. I couldn't put it off any longer.

594 I enclosed some photographs in my letter.

595 I didn't know whether to send the letter airmail or not.

596 How long does it take for a letter to get to California?

597 Don't forget to put stamps on the letter before you mail it.

598 He went to the post office to mail a letter.

599 I dropped the letter in the mailbox on the corner.

600 How did you sign the letter? Did you write, "Sincerely yours?"

UNIT **41** TELLING ABOUT PAST EXPERIENCES (과거의 일-3)

601 A strange thing happened to me morning.

602 I was crossing the street and was almost hit by a car.

603 Fortunately, I jumped back in time to avoid being hit.

604 It was a terrible experience, and I won't forget it.

605 Yesterday was such a beautiful day we decided to go for a drive.

606 We prepared a picnic lunch and drove down by the river.

607 After a while, we found a shady place under some poplar trees.

608 On the way back home, we had a flat tire.

609 It was after dark when we got back, and we were all tired.

610 I wish you would give me a more detailed description of your trip.

611 Speaking of trips, did I ever tell you about the experience I had?

612 We used to have a lot of fun when we were that age.

613 I can't recall the exact circumstances.

614 I never realized that someday I would be living in New York.

615 We never imagined that John would become a doctor.

UNIT **42** ASKING ABOUT FURNITURE AND PLACES TO LIVE (가구와 주택)

616 We're looking for a house to rent for the summer.

617 Are you trying to find a furnished house?

618 This split-level house is for rent. It's a bargain.

619 That house is for sale. It has central heating.

620 We have a few kitchen things and a dining room set.

621 This is an interesting floor plan. Please show me the basement.

622 The roof has leaks in it, and the front steps need to be fixed.

623 We've got to get a bed and a dresser for the bedroom.

624 Does the back door have a lock on it?

625 They've already turned on the electricity. The house is ready.

626 I'm worried about the appearance of the floor. I need to wax it.

627 If you want a towel, look in the linen closet.

628 What style furniture do you have? Is it traditional?

629 We have drapes for the living room, but we need kitchen curtains.

630 The house need painting. It's in bad condition.

UNIT 43 TALKING ABOUT THINGS TO WEAR (의복에 관한 대화)

631 What are you going to wear today?

632 I'm going to wear my blue suit. Is that all right?

633 I have two suits to send to the cleaners.

634 I have some shirts to send to the laundry.

635 You ought to have that coat cleaned and pressed.

636 I've got to get this shirt washed and ironed.

637 All my suits are dirty. I don't have anything to wear.

638 You'd better wear a light jacket. It's chilly today.

639 This dress doesn't fit me anymore.

640 I guess I've outgrown this pair of trouses.

641 These shoes are worn-out. They've lasted a long time.

642 I can't fasten this collar button.

643 Why don't you get dressed now? Put on your work clothes.

644 My brother came in, changed his clothes, and went out again.

645 I didn't notice you were wearing your new hat.

UNIT 44 DISCUSSING DIFFERENT POINTS OF VIEW (의견차이에 관한 토론)

646 You have your point of view, and I have mine.

647 You approach it in a different way than I do.

648 I won't argue with you, but I think you're being unfair.

649 That's a liberal point of view.

650 He seems to have a lot of strange ideas.

651 I don't see any point in discussing the question any further.

652 What alternatives do I have?

653 Everyone is entitled to his own opinion.

654 There are always two sides to everything.

655 We have opposite views on this.

656 Please forgive me. I didn't mean to start an argument.

657 I must know your opinion. Do you agree with me?

658 What point are you trying to make?

659 Our views are not so far apart, after all.

660 We should be able to resolve our differences.

UNIT **45** THINKING ABOUT POSSIBLE FUTURE ACTIVITIES (미래의 일-2)

661 If it doesn't rain tomorrow, I think I'll go shopping.

662 There's a possibility we'll go, but it all depends on the weather.

663 If I have time tomorrow, I think I'll get a haircut.

664 I hope I remember to ask the barber not to cut my hair too short.

665 My son wants to be a policeman when he grows up.

666 If I get my work finished in time, I'll leave for New York Monday.

667 Suppose you couldn't go on the trip. How would you feel?

668 What would you say if I told you I couldn't go with you?

669 If I buy that car, I'll have to borrow some money.

670 If I went with you, I'd have to be back by six o'clock.

671 One of these days, I'd like to take a vacation.

672 As soon as I can, I'm going to change jobs.

673 There's a chance he won't be able to be home for Christmas.

674 We may be able to help you in some way.

675 If you were to attend the banquet, what would you wear?

UNIT **46** TALKING ABOUT PAST POSSIBILITIES (과거의 일-4)

676 What would you have done last night if you hadn't had to study?

677 I would have gone on the picnic if it hadn't rained.

678 If you had gotten up earlier, you would have had time for breakfast.

679 If I had had time, I would have called you.

680 Would he have seen you if you hadn't waved to him?

681 If he had only had enough money, he would have bought that house.

682 I wish you had called me back the next day, as I had asked you to.

683 If you hadn't slipped and fallen, you wouldn't have broken your leg.

684 If I had known you wanted to go, I would have called you.

685 Had I known you didn't have a key, I wouldn't have locked the door.

686 She would have gone with me, but she didn't have time.

687 If I had asked for directions, I wouldn't have gotten lost.

688 Even if we could have taken a vacation, we might not have wanted to.

689 Everything would have been all right if you hadn't said that.

690 Looking back on it, I wish we hadn't given in so easily.

UNIT **47** ASKING ABOUT LIKES AND DISLIKES (좋고 싫은 것에 관한 응답)

691 What is it you don't like about winter weather?

692 I don't like it when the weather gets real cold.

693 I can't stand summer weather.

694 The thing I don't like about driving is all the traffic on the road.

695 He doesn't like the idea of going to bed early.

696 I like to play tennis, but I'm not a very good player.

697 I don't like spinach even though I know it's good for me.

698 I'm afraid you're being too particular about your food.

699 He always finds fault with everything.

700 She doesn't like anything I do or say.

701 You have wonderful taste in clothes.

702 What's your favorite pastime?

703 What did you like best about the movie?

704 I didn't like the taste of the medicine, but I took it anyway.

705 Why do you dislike the medicine so much?

UNIT **48** GIVING ADVICE AND OPINIONS (충고와 의견의 제안)

706 If you want my advice, I don't think you should go.

707 I suggest that you tear up the letter and start over again.

708 It's only a suggestion, and you can do what you please.

709 Let me give you a little fatherly advice.

710 If you don't like it. I wish you would say so.

711 Please don't take offense. I only wanted to tell you what I think.

712 In my opinions, the house isn't worth the price they're asking.

713 My feeling is that you ought to stay home tonight.

714 It's none of my business, but I think you ought to work harder.

715 In general, my reaction is favorable.

716 If you don't take my advice, you'll be sorry.

717 I've always tried not to interfere in your affairs.

718 I'm old enough to make up my own mind.

719 Thanks for the advice, but this is something I have to figure out myself.

720 He won't pay attention to anybody. You're just wasting your breath.

UNIT 49 ASKING FAVORS OF OTHER PEOPLE (도움 청하기)

721 Would you please hold the door open for me?

722 You're very kind to take the trouble to help me.

723 I wish I could repay you somehow for your kindness.

724 I'm afraid it was a bother for you to do this.

725 It wasn't any bother. I was glad to do it.

726 There's just one last favor I need to ask of you.

727 I'd be happy to help you in any way I can.

728 Would you mind giving me a push? My car has stalled.

729 Would you be so kind as to open this window for me? It's stuck.

730 If there's anything else I can do, please let me know.

731 This is the last time I'll ever ask you to do anything for me.

732 I certainly didn't intend to cause you so much inconvenience.

733 He'll always be indebted to you for what you've done.

734 Could you lend me ten dollars? I left my wallet at home.

735 I'd appreciate it if you would turn out the lights. I'm sleepy.

UNIT 50 MAKING PREPARATIONS TO TRAVEL (여행 준비)

736 I didn't realize the time had passed so quickly.

737 I've got a lot of things to do before I can leave.

738 For one thing, I've got to drop by the bank to get some money.

739 It'll take almost all my savings to buy the ticket.

740 Oh, I just remembered something! I have to apply for a passport.

741 I almost forgot to have the phone disconnected.

742 It's a good thing you reminded me to take my heavy coat.

743 I never would have thought of it if you hadn't mentioned it.

744 I'll see you off at the airport.

745 They're calling your flight now. You barely have time to make it.

746 You'd better run or you're going to be left behind.

747 Don't forget to cable to let us know you arrived safely.

748 I'm sure I've forgotten something, but it's too late now.

749 Do you have anything to declare for customs?

750 You don't have to pay any duty on personal belongings.

UNIT **51**   COUNTRIES AND NATIONALITIES (국가와 국적에 관한 표현)

751 What's your nationality? Are you American?

752 What part of the world do you come from?

753 I'm an American by birth.

754 I was born in Spain, but I'm a citizen of France.

755 Do you know what the population of Japan is?

756 What's the area of the Congo in square miles?

757 Who is the governor of this state?

758 According to the latest census, our population has increased.

759 Politically, the country is divided into fifty states.

760 The industrial area is centered largely in the north.

761 The country is rich in natural resources. It has mineral deposits.

762 This nation is noted for its economic stability.

763 How old do you have to be to vote in the national elections?

764 Today we celebrate our day of independence. It's a national holiday.

765 My home is in the capital. It's a cosmopolitan city.

UNIT **52**   GEOGRAPHY AND LAND FEATURES (지리와 지협)

766 Geographically, this country is located in the southern hemisphere.

767 It's a beautiful country with many large lakes.

768 This part of the country is very mountainous.

769 The land in this region is dry nd parched.

770 Along the northern coast there are many high cliffs.

771 There are forests here, and lumbering is important.

772 The scenery is beautiful near the Pacific Ocean.

773 This mountain range has many high peaks and deep canyons.

774 What kind of climate do you have? Is it mild?

775 How far is it from the shore of the Atlantic to the mountains?

776 Is the coastal plain good for farming?

777 What's the longest river in the United States?

778 Are most of the lakes located in the north central region?

779 As you travel westward, does the land get higher?

780 The weather is warm and sunny here. Do you get much rain?

UNIT 53 SCHOOLS AND EDUCATION (학교와 교육)

781 Children enter school at the age of five, don't they?

782 In elementary school, the child learns to read and write.

783 In secondary school, children get more advanced knowledge.

784 In universities, students train to become teachers and engineers.

785 He went to grade school in New York and high school in Chicago.

786 In college I majored in science. What was your major?

787 My sister graduated from high school. Graduation was last night.

788 I'm a graduate of Yale University. I have a bachelor of Arts degree.

789 If you expect to enter the university, you should apply now.

790 This is my first year of college. I'm a freshman.

791 My uncle is a high school principal.

792 What kind of grades did you make in college?

793 During your first year of college, did you make straight A's?

794 My brother is a member of the faculty. He teaches economics.

795 John has extracurricular activities. He's on the football team.

UNIT 54 WORK AND CAREERS (일과 직장)

796 I'm federal employee. I work for the Department of Labor.

797 What kind of work do you do? Are you a salesman?

798 As soon as I complete my training, I'm going to be a bank teller.

799 John has built up his own business. He owns a hotel.

800 What do you want to be when you grow up? Have you decided yet?

801 I like painting, but I wouldn't want it to be my life's work.

802 Have you ever thought about a career in the medical profession?

803 My uncle was a pilot with the airlines. He just retired.

804 My brother's in the army. He was just promoted to the rank of major.

805 I have a good-paying job with excellent hours.

806 My sister worked as a secretary before she got married.

807 George's father is an attorney. He has his own practice.

808 He always takes pride in his work. He's very efficient.

809 Mr. Smith is a politician. He's running for election as governor.

810 After a successful career in business, he was appointed ambassador.

UNIT 55 FARMS AND FACTORIES (농장과 공장)

811 Because of the warm and sunny weather, oranges grow very well here.

812 In this flat country people grow wheat and corn and raise cattle.

813 The ground around here is stony and not very good for farming.

814 What are the principal farm products in this region?

815 Milk, butter, and cheese are shipped here from the dairy farms.

816 They had to cut down a lot of trees to make room for farms.

817 At this time of the year farmers plow their fields.

818 On many farms you'll find cows and chickens.

819 If you have cows you have to get up early to do the milking.

820 Tractors have revolutionized farming.

821 In the United States, there are many factories for making cloth.

822 Factories employ both male and female workers.

823 If you work in a factory, you usually have to punch a clock.

824 Is meat packing a big industry in your country?

825 Is it true that the manufacturing of automobiles is a major industry?

UNIT 56 HOBBIES AND INTERESTS (취미와 관심사)

826 My hobby is collecting stamps. Do you have a hobby?

827 I've always thought photography would be an interesting hobby.

828 Some people like horseback riding, but I prefer golfing as a hobby.

829 Do you have any special interest other than your job?

830 Learning foreign languages is just an avocation with me.

831 I find stamp collecting relaxing and it takes my mind off my work.

832 On weekends I like to get my mind off my work by reading good books.

833 My cousin is a member of a drama club. He seems to enjoy acting.

834 He plays the piano for his own enjoyment.

835 I've gotten interested in hi-fi. I'm building my own equipment.

836 He's not a professional. He plays the piano for the fun of it.

837 I've heard of unusual hobbies, but I've never heard of that one.

838 The trouble with photography is that it's an expensive hobby.

839 That's a rare set of coins. How long did it take you to collect them?

840 I started a new hobby. I got tired of working in the garden.

UNIT 57 RECREATION AND SPORTS (오락과 스포츠)

841 Baseball is my favorite sport. What's your favorite?

842 My nephew is a baseball player. He is a catcher.

843 When you played football, what position did you play?

844 We played a game last night. The score was tied six-to-six.

845 I went to a boxing match last night. It was a good fight.

846 When I was on the track team, I used to run the quarter mile.

847 I like fishing and hunting, but I don't like swimming.

848 My favorite winter sport is skiing. I belong to a ski club.

849 Would you be interested in going to the horse races this afternoon?

850 The hardest thing to learn is to be a good loser.

851 Be a good sport. Play according to the rules of the game.

852 Our family went camping last summer. We had to buy a new tent.

853 This afternoon we went to the gym for a workout. We lifted weights.

854 What do you do for recreation? Do you have a hobby?

855 My muscles are sore from playing baseball.

UNIT 58 NEWSPAPERS AND MAGAZINES (신문과 잡지)

856 I sent in a subscription to that magazine. It's put out every week.

857 If you subscribe to the newspaper, it'll be delivered to your door.

858 I didn't read the whole paper. I just glanced at the headlines.

859 The first chapter of the story is in this issue of the magazine.

860 I haven't seen the latest issue of the magazine. Is it out yet?

861 What's the total circulation of this newspaper?

862 I'm looking for the classified section. Have you seen it?

863 My brother-in-law is a reporter on The New York Times staff.

864 There was an article in today's paper about the election.

865 There wasn't much news in the paper today.

866 How long have you been taking this magazine?

867 Did you read the article about the rescue of the two fishermen?

868 Why don't you put an advertisement in the paper to sell your car?

869 I got four replies to my ad about the bicycle for sale.

870 My son has a newspaper route. He delivers the morning paper.

UNIT 59 RADIO AND TELEVISION (라디오와 텔레비전)

871 What channel did you watch on television last night?

872 I don't get a good picture on my TV set. There's something wrong.

873 You get good reception on your radio.

874 Please turn the radio up. It's too low.

875 What's on following the news and weather? Do you have a TV guide?

876 You ought to have Bill look at your TV. Maybe he could fix it.

877 We met one of the engineers over at the television station.

878 Where can I plug in the TV? Is this outlet all right?

879 I couldn't hear the program because there was too much static.

880 your car radio works very well. What kind is it?

881 The next time I buy a TV set, I'm going to buy a portable model.

882 I wonder if this is a local broadcast.

883 You'd get better TV reception if you had an outside antenna.

884 Most amateur radio operators build their own equipment.

885 Station WRC is off the air now. They signed off two hours ago.

UNIT 60 MUSIC AND LITERATURE (음악과 문학)

886 What's your favorite kind of music? Do you like jazz?

887 He's a composer of serious music. I like his music a lot.

888 We went to a concert last night to hear the symphony orchestra.

889 My brother took lessons on the trumpet for nearly ten years.

890 You play the piano beautifully. How much do you practice every day?

891 I've never heard that piece before. Who wrote it?

892 Have you ever thought about becoming a professional musician?

893 Who is the author of this novel?

894 I've never read a more stirring story.

895 Who would you name as the greatest poet of our times?

896 This poetry is realistic. I don't care for it very much.

897 Many great writers were not appreciated fully while they were alive.

898 This is a poem about frontier life in the United States.

899 This writer uses vivid descriptions in his writings.

900 How much do you know about the works of Henry Wads worth Longfellow?

7. Assignment Sheet

(숙제 답안지)

1. Spoken American English : Tape #1

Dept._____ No._____ Name._____ Class._____

Assignment Sheet

2. Spoken American English : Tape #2

Dept._____ No._____ Name._____ Class._____

3. Spoken American English : Tape #4

Dept._____ No._____ Name._____ Class._____

3. Spoken American English : Tape #4

4. Spoken American English : Tape #5

Dept._____ No._____ Name._____ Class._____

Assignment Sheet

4. Spoken American English : Tape #5

5. Hunting for English (2) : Video 1-6~10

Dept._____ No._____ Name._____ Class._____

6. Hunting for English (2) : Video 2-6~10

Dept._____ No._____ Name._____ Class._____

7. Hunting for English (2) : Video 3-6~10

Dept._____ No._____ Name._____ Class._____

8. Hunting for English (2) : Video 4-5~9

Dept._____ No._____ Name._____ Class._____

9. Hunting for English (2) : Video 5-4~8

Dept._____ No._____ Name._____ Class._____

10. Hunting for English (2) : Video 6-5~9

Dept._____ No._____ Name._____ Class._____

Assignment Sheet

11. Hunting for English (2) : Video 7-4~8

Dept._____ No._____ Name._____ Class._____

12. Hunting for English (2) : Video 8-5~9

Dept._____ No._____ Name._____ Class._____

13. Hunting for English (2) : Video 9-6~10

Dept._____ No._____ Name._____ Class._____

14. Hunting for English (2) : Video 10-6~10

Dept._____ No._____ Name._____ Class._____

Assignment Sheet

Actual English Workbook

2015년 2월 10일 초판 1쇄 발행
2018년 8월 10일 초판 3쇄 발행

지은이　　이 석 만
펴낸이　　임 순 재

펴낸곳　　(주)도서출판 **한올출판사**
등　록　　제11-403호
주　소　　서울특별시 마포구 모래내로 83(성산동, 한올빌딩 3층)
전　화　　(02)376-4298(대표)
팩　스　　(02)302-8073
홈페이지　　www.hanol.co.kr
e-메일　　hanol@hanol.co.kr

값 12,000원　　　ISBN 979-11-5685-052-6